CAPT. ELKANA (KUNO) COHEN

OCT 7

THE WAR AGAINST HAMAS THROUGH THE EYES OF AN ISRAELI COMMANDO OFFICER

VIVA
EDITIONS

Published in the United States by Viva Editions, an imprint of Start Midnight, LLC, 221 River Street, Ninth Floor, Hoboken, New Jersey 07030.

Printed in the United States
Cover design: Liron Maliah
Text design: Sarit Rozenberg
Translation: Sara Hadas and Shimshon Ben Avraham

First Edition.

10 9 8 7 6 5 4 3 2 1

Trade paper ISBN: 978-1-63228-104-3
E-book ISBN: 978-1-63228-112-8

For security reasons, the names of some individuals and locations have been changed throughout the book.

CAPT. ELKANA (KUNO) COHEN

OCT 7

Table of Contents:

"The persona of the Israeli officer who strives for absolute victory is well reflected in Capt. Elkana Cohen's new book"

> Prime Minister Benjamin Netanyahu at the Officers Course graduation ceremony on March 7, 2024

"Elkana Cohen tells the story of thousands of young reservists who dropped everything on October 7th and went out to defend our nation"

> Naftali Bennett, 13th Prime Minister of Israel, on the evening of the original book launch, February 24, 2024

"As Kuno's comrade, I feel the book accurately and impressively reflects our shared experiences and the resilient spirit that fueled us. The book connects readers directly to the reality of the fighters in Gaza, just as it truly was. Even though I fought alongside Kuno and we experienced the war together, this book completely captivated me, and moved me to the point where I couldn't put it down. It brought back vivid memories of all the significant events and experiences we shared. I highly recommend this book!"

> Avri Meir, Teammate

Preface

One of my missions in life is to support and rally the troops who fight for liberty and freedom—patriotic heroes who lay their lives on the line protecting democracy and our Judeo-Christian way of life. Israeli Defense Forces Captain Elkana Cohen is one of those heroes.

His dedication to serving and protecting the people of Israel is remarkable, and his fascinating diary paints a vivid picture of his time fighting Hamas in Gaza. Very few books capture what it's really like to step into a soldier's boots and fight terrorists in an urban landscape. Captain Cohen transports the reader to the battlefield and illustrates the painstaking lengths IDF soldiers go to protect innocent lives, while focusing on their main objective—destroying Hamas.

October 7, 2023, changed everything for Israelis and the civilized world. If it weren't for great men like Elkana Cohen, Israel would be in the hands of the terrorists and the world would be in greater danger.

Mark R. Levin

Introduction

I only started writing this diary on my eighth day of being in Gaza: Monday, November 6. I realized that this was an extraordinary event. It was a historic moment, and I knew that if I didn't write it down, I probably wouldn't remember most of what I experienced. From that day forward, I made sure to write at every possible moment. When I had no time, I made time. Writing became an inseparable part of the war. At night, when my comrades went to sleep, I stayed up to write. I would carry a notebook and pen in my vest on every mission. When I had no time to write, I would jot down some bullet points and come back to my notebook and elaborate when things calmed down. There were times when writing became my place for venting and processing experiences. At other times, it became a burden, another mission, and I would tell myself, "you started this, you gotta finish it!" Sometimes, writing meant that I couldn't join my comrades when they sat down together to eat and chat.

For me, writing and documenting has great significance. This is because the Swords of Iron[1] War is an integral part of Israel's history, and my generation – the generation that went

---

1   This is the official Israeli name for the war started by Hamas on October 7, 2023.

to fight in Gaza – is another link in the chain that stretches back to the War of Independence.

Seventy-five years ago, David Ben-Gurion stood and spoke before the Provisional State Council. Just two months after the Declaration of Independence, the official agenda of public representatives was strikingly similar to that of their successors today. They started with questions of salaries in the Israel Police and continued with a discussion about the composition of the Supreme Court. But Ben-Gurion's speech was different; he came to deliver a situational assessment of the ongoing War of Independence. He began his address with the similarities and differences between this war and the biblical wars of Israel, and then said:

> "I hope that the day will come – and it is not far off – when it will be possible to tell the details of the great and wonderful tale; of how the Jewish forces, those who fought this battle, were established, organized, equipped, trained, and armed. For now, I will mention just one secret weapon, which, more than anything else, has contributed to our standing and our victories over the past eight months. It is this: the spirit of the Jew, of the Jewish pioneer and the Jewish soldier, the spirit of vision and faith and devotion, which beats in the hearts of our youth, in the hearts of our inhabitants, and in the heart of our army. Through the strength of this spirit we have, over the course of seventy years, built souls – the soul of man and of land, and created an economy, culture and Jewish fortitude. Through this spirit, we have been victorious thus far. And if we

encounter a military challenge once again, I believe wholeheartedly that we will prevail."

On Saturday, October 7, 2023, we woke up to the sounds of sirens heralding the outbreak of Israel's Second War of Independence. The day will come when it will be possible to tell the details of this war: a war which began with an agonizing failure, and which must end with a resounding victory. My war diary, which you are now holding in your hands, is my first attempt at conveying my experiences, as a combat soldier in the Gaza Strip.

I felt that special spirit of the Israeli soldier, of which David Ben-Gurion spoke, up close, day and night; it is what held us together in moments of uncertainty and of longing, when facing fire and in moments of fear. It manifested itself in the bravery of our dear friends who fell in battle, and in the clenched jaws of those who continued to fight, despite everything. It's the spirit of all those for whom 10/7/23 became a personal ID number that I'm trying to convey in the pages of this diary. So that we may never forget what happened and even more importantly, so that we may draw the strength from such an experience to build a better and safer future.

On Simchat Torah we redefined the significant and the insignificant, the urgent and the trivial, the essential and the superfluous. When I left Gaza for the first time and looked into the faces of those who fought alongside me, I knew that we were moving from one war to another. From a war of destruction against the enemy to a war of rebuilding, together with our brothers inside Israel. We have a new social contract to write, one which will express our shared vision for the next seventy years. We have a new leadership approach to establish, one which will raise the banner of accountability. We have a new military strategy to formulate, one which will address the very real threats to our lives with honesty and directness. We have a lot of work ahead of us. Writing this diary was the first step of my journey. I hope that reading it will inspire you to join our collective endeavor.

During the war, I had the privilege of meeting and getting to know hundreds of good people whose only goal was to care for us and make our lives easier. Unfortunately, I do not remember them all, but I know they did not act out of a desire to be remembered or to be written about, but rather to cheer, strengthen, and encourage the soldiers who were fighting. I promise you that you achieved this, and with great success. I want to first and foremost thank Racheli, Luli (Ella) Enoch, and Halit Navot who helped us to no end. I don't have enough words to express my gratitude. You taught me the meaning of devotion, boundless giving, and hospitality. Thank you for the long period in which you endlessly took care of our food, laundry, equipment, and many other things, all with a smile.

To the amazing people who never left us, cooked for us, washed our laundry, donated their money, accompanied and performed for us voluntarily: Roni Freeman, Rafael and Odeya Freilich, David Abargel, Noa Sabag, Shani Elgali, Erez Amosi, Negev Levy, Smadar Mishriki, Rinat Samarly,

Sharon Azriel, Hilla Rotem, R.T, Ravit Amergi and the brewer from Ra'anana, Einav Haimovich, Jacob Mitrani, Ortal Slobodin, Gilat and Naftali Bennett, the Sarfati family, Guy Elkaim, Moshe Ben Aharon, Yosi Buchnik, Ariela Atzitz, Night Cookie Ra'anana, Noam Tzurieli, Dudu Tassa, Udi Kagan, Eli Haviv, Lior Suchard, and many others.

A big thank you to all the commanders under whom I had the honor to fight. It was a great privilege for me.

Thank you from the bottom of my heart to all of my comrades. I had the privilege of joining you during the war, and was touched by how you welcomed me into your midst. Beyond the privilege of fighting alongside you, I had a constructive, powerful, and challenging experience. I learned how much strength can exist among friends, and for that, I thank you. And no less important, thank you to the partners and families of the unit. You accompanied us all the way and did so wonderfully.

Thank you very much to Dorothy and Manny Khoen who generously supported us. Our team appreciates and cherishes you to no end.

Thank you to the Bettan, Fallah, Roth, and Cohen families, mine and Shiran's extended family, who always helped, donated, and rallied for everything we could think of.

Thank you to my immediate family – Mom, Dad, Dvir and Eden, Or, Tchelet, Tzion, Dror, and Miriam.

Thank you to my dearest Meme Galia and Pepe Yitzhak. Sivan, Razi, Liel and Oriyan, Yidan, Shaked and sweet Zohar, Oren, Eden, and Eliran. Thank you to Sella-Meir Publishers for making this book possible in Hebrew.

Thank you very much to the book's editors and translators, Sara Hadas and Shimshon Ben Avraham, who helped me synthesize and publish the diary you are holding.

And last but not least, my dear Shiranush. Thank you for your bravery and the strength of your soul. For your ability to see the bright side of everything and everyone. I learned so much from you during this period. Thank you for the fact that, even in moments of difficulty and crisis, you managed to keep your head above water and fill me with strength, faith, and love.

Until victory!

Elkana (Kuno) Cohen
Ra'anana 2024

October 7, 2023: Simchat Torah

The previous evening we had eaten the holiday meal at the Bettans' house in Ra'anana, Shiran's family. It had been an extremely long day and we were utterly exhausted. When we finished the meal, it was obvious that we would stay there to sleep. Our apartment is only a fifteen minute walk away, but, given our exhaustion, that was fifteen minutes too far. We quickly fell asleep on the bed in the guest room, which is inside the safe room.[2]

At around 05:30, Shiran woke me up in a panic. "Elkana, I had a nightmare! Hundreds of terrorists infiltrated our town and chased after us and you couldn't shoot them." In my state of fatigue I mumbled to her, "Shiranush, everything's fine, you have nothing to worry about", but she insisted. I hugged her tightly and said, "Shiranush, don't worry. I'm here with you and nothing will happen to you." I fell asleep again within seconds.

At 06:30 I woke up. I struggled to open my eyes, when suddenly I realized that we were surrounded by all of Shiran's family members. "What now?" I asked in my tiredness. It turns out there had been a siren, so everyone rushed into the safe room. In the background,

---

2 Most houses and apartments in Israel have a reinforced safe room, which is purpose-built to withstand a direct rocket attack.

one could hear the never-ending noises of the Iron Dome's[3] interceptions, but I tried not to let the commotion affect me too much, for, after all, the rule famously states that the moment you open your eyes and start talking, your chances of falling asleep decrease drastically.

I turned over in bed, hugged Shiran, and continued to sleep. At around 07:30 I woke up again. I rubbed my eyes to check that I wasn't dreaming and that there were indeed the sounds of more sirens and interceptions. I don't normally get worked up by such things, because unfortunately we live in a country where this has become routine. But usually, each "round" comes after a specific incident. As far as I was aware, nothing had happened before the holiday started, so there was no reason that something unusual should start… and numerous missile launches towards the center of the country is undoubtedly unusual. I understood we were dealing with something serious.

This time, I woke up and ran home to turn on my phone to check if something had happened and if I was needed. I arranged with Shiran to meet at the synagogue, because after all, we had no doubt that the prayer services and the Hakafot[4] would be proceeding as usual. I ran as fast as I could, dressed in my Shabbat pants, a knit shirt, and flip-flops. On the way, I passed people on the street with

---

3   An Israeli air-defense system which intercepts rockets by firing multiple missiles at the incoming projectile, resulting in a loud boom.

4   A ritual performed on Simchat Torah – a holiday which celebrates completing the year-long Torah reading cycle – where Torahs are paraded around the synagogue in a celebratory fashion.

frightened looks in their eyes. I asked them if they knew what happened, and they replied that they had heard there was "lots of chaos in the South." There was a feeling of war, even when we knew nothing. Something about Shiran's dream, the sirens, and the general foreboding atmosphere pushed me to run faster.

When I arrived home, I called Yossi, the deputy commander of the Commando Brigade. I don't have a combat role in my regular reserve duty, but rather I'm responsible for helping combat soldiers to process their experiences and for overseeing tryouts for the Commando Brigade, so I don't belong to any unit that would be called up during war. But it was clear to me that if a war broke out I would find a way to participate, and I waited for Yossi to answer.

"Hey Kuno, how are you?" he asks and I cut him off: "Yossi, I have no idea what's going on right now in the South, I haven't seen the news or anything. But know that I'm joining you. If you need a combat soldier, I'll be there." Yossi responds, "Listen, Kuno, I also have no idea what's going on there right now, get your gear ready and I'll let you know as soon as I have more details. Thanks for calling".

I hadn't even hung up the call when I received a call from Gabi, a friend who had been with me in my unit and who now served with Shiran. "Kuno, get me Shiran! We need her in the unit!" "What happened?" I asked him. "Kuno, it's terrible! There are trucks of terrorists in Sderot. They've kidnapped a soldier!" I couldn't believe it. Kidnapped a soldier?! I promised Gabi that as soon as I got my equipment in order I'd pick up Shiran.

Organizing my equipment, I heard knocks on the door and I shouted "yes!" while taking care to fill my hydration pack. Dolev came in. He looks at me and laughs, "What happened to you, have you gone crazy? What are you doing?" Our living room was covered in uniforms, military equipment, magazines, and anything that might come in useful in combat. Dolev and I have a tradition – every Shabbat or holiday morning we meet at my place for an iced coffee and a good cake that we make sure to bake in advance.

He laughs and I laugh. "Do you really have no idea, Doli"? I was sure he was joking around.

"Are you going to tell me what's going on?", he asks, and I realize he's serious.

"Listen to me, Dolev, they're talking about war! Didn't you hear the Iron Dome interceptions this morning?"

"What interceptions? I slept like a baby!"

"There were loads!" I tell him, without mentioning that if Shiran's family hadn't woken me up, I probably would've still been asleep... "Basically, get ready, we're headed for war. They've also called up Shiran."

I finished packing, and as always, prepared us each an iced coffee and a thick slice of yeast cake that Shiran baked. After we finished eating and drinking, we wished each other luck. Dolev serves in one of the operational teams in Maglan,[5] and it was only a matter of time before they'd call him too. We concluded, "Until the next coffee." We got up and hugged. I put on my uniform,

---

5   An elite commando unit.

took my gun, and drove to the synagogue. When I arrived, I left the car running and ran to the women's section. Some of the women started crying and getting emotional, and I could hear wishes of "may God watch over you" all around. I explained the situation to Shiran and told her that we'd been called up, and that we needed to get to the unit as fast as possible. In the synagogue, they were in the middle of the holiday Torah reading for Simchat Torah. I stood on the side, prayed quickly, and got ready to leave. Everyone blessed us that we may go in peace and return in peace.

We parted from Shiran's family with a big hug. Seeing how hard it was for Galia, Shiran's mother, I have to admit that I was filled with some pride. Here we are, a couple going together to reserve duty. There's something touching and special about it. Shiran quickly prepared her equipment, and we were on our way.

It's a strange feeling, driving in a car together during a holiday and Shabbat. Looking back, I can say that in the months that followed, observing Shabbat became a strange feeling in general. In any case, we moved towards the Duvdevan[6] army base.

When we arrived, I noticed how many people had dropped everything to come straight to the unit. Hundreds of cars were blocking the entrance to the base and dozens of soldiers were standing at the entrance, arguing with the guard to let them in.

We all shared the same feeling: it didn't matter that we hadn't received a call up to reserve duty – we are taking part

---

6   An elite commando unit.

in this war. One of the HR officers tells me, "Listen, we don't have any more equipment to give you, we already have over 180% enlistment." I nodded at her in understanding, quickly parted from Shiran, went around the officer, and entered the base. I made sure to put my ranks on my uniform, hoping that being a lieutenant might somehow help me in the current situation.

I started trying to gather equipment. I needed a vest, helmet, knee pads, and – most importantly – a weapon. When I approached the warehouses, they told me "Sorry, but we can't give anything out. You should go back home because you won't find any combat equipment here." A wave of frustration washed over me. The entire south was ablaze, and I wouldn't be able to take part in the fighting just because of some equipment shortage?!

I went to one of Duvdevan's special units, thinking I might be able to find a guy there with spare equipment. I bumped into Etan Naeh, a good friend I hadn't seen in a while. I was very happy to see him. We chatted for a few minutes, and when I hugged him goodbye, I said with a smile, "Etan, no silly business, ok? No shenanigans or playing the hero!" Etan smiled, and I continued racking my brain to work out where I could go to get equipment.

Suddenly an idea popped into my head. There's a building on the base called "Duvdevan House" which is divided in two: one room dedicated to soldier-commander meetings and debriefs and the second part's entire purpose is to display our badass equipment and to raise funds for the unit. When I served in the unit, there had been a display mannequin that stood in the Duvdevan House, dressed like a combat soldier with all the latest models: vest, helmet, knee pads, gloves, and – the pièce de résistance – tactical uniforms. In short, I rushed (all the while careful not to arouse suspicion) to the Duvdevan House to check if my memory had served me correctly, and indeed, to my delight, the mannequin was standing there wearing all the equipment. Pleased with myself and proud of my ingenious idea, I left the building with a full set of equipment. I glanced all around to make sure no one had caught me and headed towards the synagogue to inspect the equipment thoroughly. I was disappointed to discover that the mannequin's tactical helmet was made of plastic, but aside from the helmet, the rest of the equipment was excellent. Now all that was left to do was to sign for a weapon and find a team that would accept me. After all kinds of delays, I joined one of Duvdevan's reserve units.

A few hours later, they gathered us together in the Duvdevan House to give an update on the situation and to set some order amidst all the chaos. Shiran and I sat next to each other, it was nice. The mannequin and I exchanged glances, keepers of a secret. "What's so funny?" Shiran asked curiously. "Nothing!" I replied, "I'm just happy to be sitting here next to you." Shiran wouldn't have been too thrilled with the whole mannequin affair, and besides, the mannequin and I had a secret agreement – I couldn't betray it.

We concluded the briefing and I was getting my final pieces of equipment ready when suddenly I got a call from Yemini, a friend from the unit. "What's up, Kuno, where are you?"

I explained to him that I was at the base and seemed to have joined one of the commando squads.

"Cut the bullshit," Yemini shouts through the phone. "Come join the team. We're stationed under the 551st Brigade, they just called us up to the emergency depots in Bilu, we'd really love for you to join!"

He didn't need to persuade me too much. It felt natural to rejoin the team. I hadn't served with them since the end of the unit's training course, but of course, if there was a war, it could only be fought with my team!

I signed off on the weapon and spoke to Shiran. Evening had already fallen. It was hard for her to think of me going with the team, and she was scared we'd end up fighting in Gaza. Something about me being by her side on the base had provided her with some peace of mind. I explained that I had to be there, that this was my place, and she had nothing to worry about. I gave her a hug, we said Havdallah[7] together, and parted ways. As I left, I called Or, my brother who had also served in Duvdevan and who had been discharged just two months ago.

"Orchook, what's up? Where are you? Are you on your way to the unit? Were you called up?"

"Hey Elka, how are you doing? Yes, I'm just getting to the base now."

"Damn, I can't believe I just missed you, what a bummer. Anyway, give my love to Shiran, it's nice that you two will be there together. Love you, brother. Take care of yourself."

---

7   A ceremony performed at the end of Shabbat and Holidays, marking the end of the special day and the start of a regular one.

"I love you too, Elkush. Take care of yourself, and don't worry about Shiran, I'm here."

I typed "Bilu Junction" into Waze and headed towards the team. Nothing was clear in the chaotic situation we found ourselves in. I didn't know where terrorists might pop out from, so I drove wearing a vest and knee pads, with an old helmet I found next to me, and a handgun between my legs, ready for any trouble that might come my way.

On the way, I remembered Saba Chaim. Every year, I help my grandfather build his sukkah[8] after Yom Kippur and take it down after Simchat Torah. I told myself I had to stop by his place in Mevaseret Tzion and help him dismantle the sukkah. It would only take me a few minutes, and Mevaseret Tzion is relatively on the route to Bilu anyway. At the time, I didn't fully understand the extent of what was happening on the Gaza border, so there was no reason not to stop by for a couple of minutes. Without any warning, I showed up at my grandparents' doorstep dressed in army uniform and combat gear. "Shavua tov,"[9] I announced loudly. My grandmother, seeing me come in wearing uniform and gear, became emotional.

"Nani, what are you doing here?" she asked, surprised.

"I was called up to Bilu, but I couldn't give up the honor of helping Grandpa with the sukkah," I replied.

"Oh Nani, you really don't need to! We'll manage it. We're so touched that you came."

---

8   A hut that Jews eat and sometimes even sleep in during the holiday of Sukkot.

9   Literally "Have a good week", this is the traditional greeting after Shabbat and Holidays.

You probably need to know Savta Batsheva to understand how to read that sentence in her intonation, but for me, hearing it was everything. Of course I'd stop by their house, it's truly an honor for me. Saba Chaim, who joined us in the living room, seemed surprised too. I told them, "I don't have much time, so let's start taking down the sukkah."

Within ten minutes, I had taken down, packed up, and tied the schach.[10] The rest of the dismantling would be easy for Grandpa. I asked my grandparents for a blessing and went on my way. Grandma made sure to send me off with a heavenly glass of orange juice. Sweaty and pleased with the great privilege that had come my way, I drove towards Bilu.

I took advantage of the time to make some calls. I called my mom, who was in the middle of an important conference in the United States. I knew it was still the holiday there, but it was important for me to tell her not to worry and that we were fine. I then spoke with my brother Dvir, who served as a fighter in Egoz,[11] and asked how he was. He told me that both he and Eden, his wife, were called up to reserves, Dvir to the north and she to her special unit's base. We really are a military family. I told him too how much I loved him and to take care of himself. I also managed to receive a blessing from my dad and to update Shiran's family that we were fine.

It was only when I arrived at Camp Bilu, "Camp Lipkin," that I understood the magnitude of the draft. A convoy of

10 The roof of a Sukkah, usually made of branches, bamboo, or leaves.
11 An elite commando unit.

vehicles stretched several kilometers from the base, and thousands of people were there distributing food, treats, and other good things. I parked on the pavement in front of the bus station at the entrance to the base, and entered on foot. I felt it had been a long time since I'd been in a place so crowded with people. Everyone was running around getting combat gear ready. It was as if the end of the world was near. Some of the guys were walking with a detached look in their eyes, but for others, it was a social gathering. Everyone was in their own world.

Along the way, I bump into many friends, praying for their safety. I try to imprint as many memories from each person as I can. I'm naturally optimistic, but something about this situation makes me start to worry about my friends. I'm not so worried about myself. I told Shiran before leaving that everyone has a role and mission in the world, and until you've fulfilled it, you stay here. I feel like I still have so much to do, so it's too early for me to go. At least that's what I tell myself, to instill some confidence in myself.

I arrived at the battalion's depots, where I met the whole team. How exciting. It had been a long time since I'd seen them all. I already had most of the gear, so I only had to sign for a weapon. Time flies. It's very cold outside, and we don't have rooms to sleep in. Rotem, the company commander, gives us a company-wide briefing, and we get ready to sleep. Air Force planes are flying overhead. The sounds of bombings and iron dome interceptions can be heard constantly.

It was a terrible night; I barely slept. A fear of war crept into me. It's here, and it's our turn this time. Nobody else will do it for us, and I'm not even sure I want anyone to switch with me.

And so we entered a three-week waiting period. The pre-battle period was accompanied by a spectrum of emotions: tears, happiness, anger, fear, power, mission. And the team simply knows how to contain it all. Everyone lends support and a shoulder, including you. Sometimes you're on top, sometimes below.

One of the important things I realized during the pre-battle period is that often when you're in a stressful situation, say a call-up or mission, it's hard for you to function; you can find yourself staring at the gear not knowing how to organize it. But it's very easy to help a friend. You can help them with the exact thing that you need, and what seems impossible for you becomes easy for a friend. I turned it into a rule. When it's hard for you – help others, and no less important, learn to ask them for help. This will make it much easier for you to cope.

This state of war brings up a lot of thoughts and reminds you of the people who are truly important. Even those you haven't seen for a long time. There were all sorts of people I met and got to know during the pre-battle period. I'm really glad I remembered them. I think the pre-battle period was a very important part of the fight. We were able to train a lot and sharpen our skills as fighters. From a professional perspective, I feel like a better combat soldier than I was in my mandatory service. Beyond that, it has made me a more collected and alert soldier.

We had many more experiences and kind people who

helped us: with equipment, laundry, food, and anything we needed. Thanks to them, we entered the war with lots of strength, capabilities, and energy. So many things happened during the pre-battle period, but in order to write in real-time (my eighth day in Gaza), I need to be concise.

First Notebook

Battle – Beit Hanoun

Sunday Evening, the First Day of Battle, October 29, 2023

1st Outing

Departure by bus from Bror Hayil towards Or HaNer, close to the Strip. A good atmosphere, we sing on the bus together with the Atzitz unit. There's a great vibe, the driver is being a bit annoying. We arrive at Or HaNer, from there we load up the equipment. I had a camping trolley that the Navot family had given us. I decided to attach the trolley to my belt so I could drag my heavy bag during the walk. I couldn't find a rope, so I used the power cord from a broken toaster I found nearby. It was ingenious! With hindsight, I didn't even realize how much it would help me. Some guys gave me strange looks, but I'm sure inside they were thinking to themselves, "What a brilliant idea."

We walked up to Kibbutz Erez, and this was the first time we saw the destroyed fence. This zigzagging, between exercises and laughter and the realization that we're actually at war – isn't always simple. Suddenly, there was a feeling that we could be attacked from any direction. A soldier stood with piles of water bottles and distributed them to us with a sullen look. There was the quiet and heavy atmosphere of a funeral home, the moment of farewell before death. One of the guys next to us had some kind of panic attack and was sent back.

To deal with the tension, I found it easier to stay active and engaged. I took a six-pack of water from the guy and placed it on my makeshift trolley, taking advantage of the fact that I couldn't really feel its weight to carry more water for the guys. We crossed the border with a mixture of fear and pride, and I joked that now we can "check off" Gaza in our passports. Throughout our walk on the path, I made sure to keep giving water and sweets to my friends so they wouldn't get dehydrated. That's how we walked from the border crossing up to the outskirts of Beit Hanoun, to the battalion's stronghold. A path of around 6 kilometers. The trolley was with me all the time. The bag lay in the trolley and thanks to it, I managed to stay alert and effectively walk through a warzone the whole way.

The journey was accompanied by feelings of mission, fear, and faith in the righteousness of our path. Every few hundred meters: stop, take cover, and return fire.

Monday, October 30, 2023

We arrived at the battalion's stronghold, where we quickly grasped the strength of the IDF and the extent of destruction in Beit Hanoun. During our stay at the stronghold, we suddenly spotted a drone above us. I shouted "Drone!" and the whole team took cover. We spent half a minute attempting to find out if the drone belonged to our forces.

The moment there was no answer, I initiated fire towards the drone, followed by the whole company, with hundreds of bullets whizzing over my head. The war had started. A few days later, I learned that an enemy drone had dropped a grenade from the air onto a Duvdevan unit, and I understood that it was in the exact same place. Later, we received mortar fire in our direction, and we were asked to dig pits. We also received information about a Nukhba[12] force nearby which wanted to commit an attack. We waited a little in the stronghold for the 10th Company to complete its mission and bring us into battle. We advanced towards the "Sevivon neighborhood" of Beit Hanoun (it means a spinning top in Hebrew, that's its shape on the map) and our zone.

We moved through the streets of Beit Hanoun. On one hand, absolute silence, not a soul alive. On the other hand, relentless noise of shooting and bombings with the smell of carcasses and burning. It's amazing to see how quickly nature takes control of reality: pigeons nesting inside holes created by bombings of houses, chickens and dogs roaming inside a neighborhood grocery, a donkey splashing in the mud next to a destroyed building. We stood in front of a local school for about an hour until night fell. It made me insanely antsy, but I started to understand that in war, everything moves very slowly. I noticed that the moment darkness falls, the level of stress and panic rises. We continued to advance towards the sites that we are supposed to capture. We find a half-destroyed shack attached to a building located right

---

12 The elite Hamas commando force.

across from the site. The entire company enters the shack while we work out our mission. It was really cramped in there. Everything felt like one big mess. In the background, the sound of a D9[13] engine and the smell of fuel. After the explanations, we started the battle: the Eshel team leads and we, the Nahman team, right behind them, discover a site full of Hamas equipment, weapons, and intelligence. From there, we continue to scan and clear adjacent positions. The moment we finished scanning, an IED suddenly detonated, and the shack that we had sat in an hour earlier exploded completely. It was a huge miracle.

At night we created a guarding position for the first time – adapting the building to our operational needs: blacking out windows, setting up noise-making kits, marking cardinal directions on the walls. It's hard to keep watch at night, you very quickly doze off. I made myself a "routine": every time I doze off, I do 10 squats, and wake up for a few more minutes. Throughout the night, our building was shot at a few times, but it was seemingly just peripheral shooting.

Tuesday, October 31, 2023

We wake up in the morning and get organized; there's a fire outside our reconnaissance point. It's hard to breathe, luckily I made sure to put a few breathing masks in my vest before we left. They told us we're leaving the stronghold.

---

13 A large military bulldozer.

We destroyed the entire stronghold and just at that moment they told us that in the end we were staying in the stronghold. We were extremely bummed. We went back to sleep – and suddenly, a crazy explosion! A tank stationed next to us fired a shell toward a group of terrorists without informing us. In a moment, as Nahman put it, we went from sleeping to "saving our faces" the fastest he's ever seen. We woke up and got started on our tasks. We were told that we needed to advance and clear the entire western strip.

It was a very busy day, and I don't remember everything. One of the times we searched a house, I began scanning the closets. I turned over every dresser and every sofa. The guys on the team started making fun of me, saying I was going overboard, and at one stage even got annoyed with me. "Kuno, relax! Everything's fine," said Omer, while I was going through the wardrobe in the bedroom. I found a medical certificate. The guys said, "See, Kuno? He's a doctor. It's all fine, let it go already." I didn't give up. Suddenly, I found a green Hamas headband. This was all the motivation I needed. I kept going through the closet until I started finding Kalashnikov magazines, tactical walkie-talkies. "Guys, he's a Hamas member!" I tell them. Shlomi and Omer, who were sitting on the bed in the room, stared at me with a look of surprise. "Come on, get up," I urged them. "Let's turn this house over." Amitai suggested that we move the bed. To our astonishment, we found a massive IED. Two missiles, each 1.5 meters-long, connected to a two-wire cable, with four 120mm mortar bombs lying next to them.

Later, when we talked to the engineering department who were there with us, we found out that the bomb had been supposed to explode during our search, and somehow, miraculously, nothing happened. Looking back, I can say that this event greatly impacted our conduct during the battle. Moreover, in the discussions we had after our reserve duty as part of a workshop to process our experiences, I understood that for many members of our team, this had been a defining event. We found a lot more Hamas combat equipment. From there, we moved about 200 meters eastward to blow up the IED we found in another house. There was a huge explosion, and the house was completely destroyed. It was a big miracle that it didn't hit us.

After we made sure to detonate the bomb, we went back to the adjacent site, which we took over for setting up a new stronghold. I feel that we are learning to set up a stronghold better than the previous night. There were many warnings about terrorists in the area and a lot of gunfire and bombings from the air force. Nahman gave a night briefing, and we went to sleep.

Wednesday, November 1, 2023

We woke up in the morning. The night passed well except for a comrade's hydration pack that exploded and got my equipment wet. Rotem, the company commander, wanted to start to take the western areas of Beit Hanoun, so that we could control it with our fire and observe the main path located west of us. He orders Zev, a fighter from the Atzitz team, to throw a grenade from our site to the western area, while he pushes for everyone to take cover. I tell Rotem that he himself isn't in a safe position, and he yells at me, "Kuno, get behind a cover and shut up!" A second after Zev throws the grenade, I hear Rotem scream, "Is there a medic here?" and it turns out that he got a piece of shrapnel in his back. I didn't want to say, "You deserved it," but I won't lie, it crossed my mind.

We call Kaneti, the medic, to treat Rotem. Rotem looks at Kaneti and after a second of hesitation tells him, "Leave it, I'll manage." I joked that Rotem doesn't trust him, although personally, if there's one person in the company that I trust to take care of me, it's Kaneti without a shadow of a doubt. They evacuate Rotem for treatment in Israel. The Eshel team replaced us in the stronghold, and we continued to capture the western building.

Initially, the Spear (the team's forward force) takes control of the ground floor, and then they go up to capture the first floor, while the rest of the team finishes scanning and clearing the building. Yemini, Michaeli, and I are busy building positions that cover the west and control the path. We finished making an opening in the wall and setting up positions for a machine gun and another sniper. Part of the team was busy transferring the bags from the previous stronghold while we were shooting towards suspected buildings and areas where we identified hostile movements. At one time, Michaeli disassembles the mortar and gets hurt by the weapon. Blood flows down his nose. "Welcome Michaeli, the first combat casualty of the team," I declare jokingly. We begin to set up the new stronghold.

One of the rooms in the building was full of 20-liter jerry cans of olive oil. One of them spilled over Shaked, Suedi made sure to laugh at him, and we continued. When we finished building, I noticed that this time the stronghold looked like a showcase. It was amazing to see how quickly we learned to work better. Struel, Ofir, Igor, and Dani, the company's sniper team – members of the "Havir" team from the Mitkan Adam who joined us for combat – are with us on the roof and take position for distant threats. They're undoubtedly good guys. Nahman gave a night briefing, and we sat down to eat from our army rations. During the night we have 3 positions – a guard position meant to prevent entry into the building; a MAG position with two fighters that controls the west; and also a position to patrol the path beneath us that moves from south to north.

Thursday, November 2, 2023

I woke up in the morning completely exhausted. I felt that the physical exertion and the fact that we don't get regular sleep are starting to affect me. During the night guard shifts, we heard noises from the floor below us. It sounded like someone had entered the stronghold. With our hearts pounding, we went down to scan the lower floor with red lights. It was a sheep. We discussed how we needed to find a solution for all these animals. On the one hand, it hurts my heart to just kill the animals outright, but on the other hand, they might endanger us, and the sheep sounds could desensitize us, making us less alert for noises that might be coming from other sources.

In general, since we entered the Strip, I notice how many miserable and gross animals are here. I don't know exactly what's going on with the pigeons, but they look like someone inflated them. They're about two and a half times the size of pigeons in Israel. Perhaps somehow the bombings or maybe even the diseases here cause them to puff up. The same goes for sheep and chickens.

After we woke up, Nahman gave a morning briefing, we ate a communal breakfast, and then we experienced a moving moment where Meir and Nahman, each of whom had a son born last week, gave names to their sons. Today, both boys had their circumcision ceremonies, but the fathers, who weren't in Israel and so couldn't participate in their sons' circumcisions, each said a short word of Torah and talked about the names chosen they chose to give their son.

Nahman's son was named Uri Lavi, and Meir's son was named Oz Eliyahu. It was very moving. Enormous joy in the midst of a very complex situation. The names had something in common: both Meir and Nahman talked about how they wished to add light and strength to the people of Israel through their child's name. The sniper team also heard that Meir and Nahman were giving names and came down to our floor. It really was a special event. Later, we found out that Nahman's son had jaundice, so he had to "delay" the ceremony for an extra ten days until we left Beit Hanoun.

To honor the touching event, I decided to surprise the guys. On the floor below, I found a gas stove, corn kernels, olive oil, salt, and coffee, and in a short amount of time,

I came up with popcorn and hot coffee. The guys were shocked! It was truly something special and cheering in the moment. I think it also led to a mindset change amongst the team, since from that moment we realized that we could also cook, not just eat army rations. Later, we learned to use the kitchens there in a much more impressive way.

We began to learn how to improve our conditions. We found all sorts of batteries and connected them to fans so the heat of the day passed much more pleasantly. Additionally, we found two improvised weapons in the attic, and it turns out that we almost had a friendly fire incident today: another force's sniper team mistook our sniper team for terrorists, and if not for the swiftness of Avishai, Rotem's communicator, we could have found ourselves in a disastrous situation. It's lucky that Avishai prevented a tragedy. Let's just say that since then, the snipers have been unwilling to go up to the roof.

The sun starts to set, and as I've already written, as soon as there's darkness – the action begins. A lot of bombings, mortars, and terrorists shooting in short bursts and running away.

At night, we went out for an attack on a nearby site located north of us. It was a company-level attack. We gave cover fire while other teams took over and scanned the building. Initially, we provided covering fire for the building itself. Afterward, the Spear and Squad B moved to the southeast corner of the building and covered for the rest of the strip, while we moved to a new covering position. It was fun. It was the first time that we gave covering fire as needed. The company commander joined us for the mission, there was a good atmosphere. Yemini and Meir disassembled about 3.5 boxes of MAG ammo there, alongside light machine gun fire from Victor, Kaneti, and Lahad. I was mainly busy with controlling the covering fire and preparing the ammunition belts for Yemini. We finished the mission and returned to our stronghold. Nahman gave a night briefing, and we went to sleep.

Friday, November 3, 2023

We woke up, had a team breakfast, and arranged our site. Everything was beginning to stink. Initially, when we entered the building, we turned one of the rooms into a bathroom. As time passed, the smell intensified and stank up the whole place. We washed it and made sure to clean the building as much as possible.

Later, we were informed that we were going out for another mission and, at the end of the mission, we would move to a new stronghold. We packed all our bags and passed through the previous site where we slept, which now housed the Eshel and Atzitz teams. We left our bags with them and prepared to take over the new building. The breach teams from Eshel and Atzitz used an explosive frame to create an opening in the wall for the conquest. We, Squad C, stayed behind while the Spear and Squad B started to clear and capture the building. When the Spear went up to the second floor, Michaeli identified Arabic writing on one of the walls, indicating that the building was a trap, and indeed, on the lower floor, we found several IEDs. We all packed up and left the building.

Just before sunset, we remembered that Shabbat was soon approaching. We started humming and singing Shabbat songs together. There was something special about it. It's been a long time since I managed to pray normally, and here we were, starting to sing all together while sounds of gunfire and bombings whirred in the background. While we were singing and praying, we were informed that we were going to blow up a suspicious site soon. To distance ourselves from the explosion, we stopped our prayers and moved to a nearby site so we would be under a roof during the detonation. They counted down over the radio: 7... 4... 2... 1... boom! Suddenly, a block that was attached to one of the walls fell on Victor's head. "Good thing we have helmets," I thought to myself. The block fell directly onto his head and slightly hit his shoulder. It didn't injure him, but the hit certainly affected him. We referred him to the medical team, and it was decided that he should be evacuated for a medical examination in Israel.

The sun set, and we didn't have time to set up a new stronghold, so we returned to our previous one. We were annoyed that we weren't moving. Staying in the same site for several nights could expose us to the enemy. We made sure to rearrange what we could and went to sleep.

During the night, tens of Hamas illumination mortars were fired near us. You can really identify their firing because they have a unique sound–a kind of dull and deep sound during their trajectory. Occasionally, the house shook during the night due to Air Force bombings.

Shabbat, November 4, 2023

When we woke up in the morning, we said Kiddush, packed our gear, and prepared to leave. Kaneti, Oz, and I were laying on a mattress in one of the rooms when suddenly a grenade was thrown through our window. I shouted "Grenade!" and made sure Oz and Kaneti moved back while I tried to kick it outside. Moments later, we realized it wasn't a grenade at all. One of the guys from the Atzitz unit had thrown a stone at us, it was unclear why. It really annoyed me.

We started to fold all the camouflage nets from the windows and got ourselves fully organized to leave. Yemini went to throw garbage out of the window and was surprised to find ammunition belts from a Negev gun strewn on the ground in the courtyard. While we were trying to figure out how the belts got there, Nahman suddenly noticed a black bag with a shoulder-launched anti-tank missile peeking out. Wild! We've been here for several days and only just noticed this launcher now. As far as I understand, this launcher was placed in a site close to us which was bombed. But it was supposed to be used in an ambush on the corridor we had secured. After a short while, the engineering team arrived and destroyed it.

With a slight delay, we proceeded on our 450-meter movement to the battalion-wide conquest of a school located to the east of us. In reality, the school was only about 250 meters away from us, but the planned path was longer so we could travel stealthily via points already under our control. It might not sound particularly long, but the combination of heavy bags with damaged and awkward walkways made it challenging. The team prepared to storm and capture the school. Yemini and I were transferred to the Atzitz team to reinforce their breaching unit. The goal was to take over the school building and to clear it of terrorists, explosives, and terror infrastructure. It was a very large school with buildings in the shape of the letters A and F.

The mission took a while. Lots of doors were locked, and it took a while before it was decided to use explosives. Sometimes we moved into classrooms through the walls, sometimes through the hallways. I suddenly bumped into Avishai, the communication specialist, and asked him if he had the "Red," the classified phone. Just before we had turned off our cell phones and entered Gaza, I called Shiran and my Uncle Hillel to check the number of their Red Phone. I shoved the note with the numbers into my vest.

Avishai said yes! Before he could even understand what was happening, I had the phone in my hand. After a few seconds of dialing with a pounding heart, I heard a female voice answer.

"Hello?? Hi! Who is this?"

"Hi, am I speaking with Shiran?" I asked.

"Yes, who is this?" Shiran asked.

"What, don't you recognize me?!"

"Aviel?" she tried to guess.

"What, you really don't recognize me?!"

"Nani?!", Shiran started to cry out of emotion. To her credit, she was actually waiting for a call from a Shin Bet agent named Aviel.

I was so glad I managed to catch her! It was a really

emotional conversation. She told me she's been following our actions closely. It sounded like she was doing well, which gave me a lot of strength. The battery was about to die, and we were in the middle of an operation, so I had to end the call. I told her how much I loved and missed her. I disconnected the call, returned the phone to Avishai, and continued to fight.

After we finished capturing our area near the school, I noticed the guys in the team were hungry and thirsty. I called Suedi and told him that there's a kiosk full of drinks and sweets at the entrance to the school; I knew he'd be the right partner for the mission. Very quickly, we were loaded with all the good stuff, from cans of soda to chocolate bars. On the way back to the unit, I heard some of the guys identify three terrorists outside the school, inside another battalion's zone, and didn't know what to do because they didn't want to accidentally cause a friendly fire incident. I set aside the crate with the drinks and sweets and quickly ran to the classroom where the commanders were sitting to update them. When we went back to the crate, the battalion commander got angry at me for looting and stealing. To be honest, I completely disagreed with him. In my eyes, as long as it strengthens the fighters and allows them to be better soldiers, there's no moral question. Especially when we're talking about combat soldiers who hadn't eaten or drunk since the morning. Without him noticing, I vanished from his sight along with the crate.

We finished taking control of the school, and the sun started to set. While we scanned the school, we found loads of textbooks with maps of Israel. For a moment, I got excited and thought there might actually be some people interested in peace. But then I realized: there were no maps of Israel, only of Palestine – from the river to the sea. A map that unambiguously clarifies the essence of education in the Gaza Strip: no peace agreement, no land swap scheme – they want everything, without a trace of the State of Israel remaining. This isn't only Hamas's perspective, it belongs to everyone who educates their children in this way. October 7th was just the first step of their plan. I flipped through their textbooks, all filled with propaganda and incitement, but I had to cut my brief study day short because we started moving towards the new stronghold.

We got a bit angry that we were yet again setting up a stronghold at night. The guys were exhausted and hungry, but a bite of chocolate lifted our spirits. As Meir said, "Wow, this is the best chocolate of my entire life." It took us a while to decide where to position ourselves because the whole area seemed suspicious.

We waited to get our site assignments and went out to capture and clear them. There was a mortar shell at the entrance of our building. The warhead was buried in the ground, and its "tail" was sticking out. Additionally, the guys from the 697th Battalion, positioned at a site opposite us, told us that the site had a suspected explosive device but they weren't sure. We decided to scan the building and enter it. It was already very dark, and we preferred to be inside a building. We scanned quickly and started to set up the stronghold. The Kesten team was on the ground floor, and we positioned ourselves on the first floor. Everything was covered in dust, and the living room was turned upside down. Just as we started to tidy the place up, we noticed a small hole in the ceiling. We didn't pay much attention to it initially, but a few minutes later, when we moved the table in the living room, we saw the remains of the mortar that had penetrated through the roof, which is most likely what made the apartment look the way it did.

We were tired, but the whole team was mobilized for the mission, so the entire process of setting up the stronghold went relatively smoothly. I was responsible for blacking out some of the windows, building toilets with Oz, and using the kitchen. The smells coming out of the refrigerators here are horrendous. Imagine a fridge, full of meat and everything, left closed without electricity for a month. We cautiously moved the fridge and prayed that the fridge door wouldn't accidentally swing open. It seems my prayers weren't really heard, because just a moment later I found myself cleaning a thick and stinky liquid off my shoes.

After the kitchen, we moved onto the toilets. There's no plumbing here so we can't use their toilets, especially since most of the time, because of the bombings, there isn't a single connected toilet remaining. Usually, we find a side room within the site, break the flooring in it, and fill pots and buckets with the sand that was underneath the flooring. We place a chair that we broke the seat of over the area with the broken tiles, and every time someone finishes relieving themselves, they cover their waste with sand from the bucket. When it comes to peeing, there are a few options: the sink, the bathtub, or in a bottle, so the smell doesn't overwhelm the house. But it only works for a short time, and after a few days, there's no way to stop the smell from taking over.

We finished setting up the stronghold. Nahman gave a night briefing. In the briefing, he went over all the positions and explained about threats, establishing terminology, and adjacent forces. We stood by the window while Nahman faced the location of the guys from the 697th Battalion in buildings to our east. He asked one of the guys to turn on a red flashlight for a second so that we could clearly identify their position. "Are you being serious?!" the guy nervously responded. "I don't want to invite an anti-tank missile directly to our door." I don't know why but we burst into laughter. It was the joke of the evening. We made Havdallah, and we began to get ready for bed.

Suddenly, I was hit by an awful "prickly heat." For those lucky enough not to be familiar with it, it's an infection or sores that cause an awful sensation of itching and pins and needles. The combination of the vest, sand, sweat, and lack of showers and basic hygiene is the perfect recipe for prickly heat, and it was terrible. I had pins and needles all over my body, especially on my back. I've had prickly heat a few times in my life, but this was undoubtedly the worst of them. I got to the point where I just yanked off my vest, took my shirt off, and asked a friend to clean my back. It didn't really help. Fortunately, I found some shampoo in the bathroom and used four bottles of water for a quick and very necessary shower. It worked wonders! I changed clothes and went to sleep.

Sunday, November 5, 2023

It's 09:00 in the morning. The night shifts passed relatively quickly. Yemini and I had some good chats. The night was relatively quiet. There was an alert about a sniper and enemy drones in the area. Later, I discovered that my uncle Hillel tried to meet me during the night, but he turned back because of the alerts. It was a shame, it would have been really nice to see him.

After I woke up, I prayed and prepared jugs of coffee and tea for everyone. We arranged our stronghold a bit better, and Nahman went out for the "officers' meeting." I took advantage of the available time to get a few things done.

First, I decided to level up our whole cooking situation. In the kitchen, I found two cans of tomato paste, spices, two packets of pasta and dried hot pepper, and I made pasta with spicy tomato sauce. The guys ate, and we brought the leftovers to the Kesten team. Everyone seemed happy with the food. Next, I washed yesterday's dirty uniforms and hung them up to dry.

When Nahman returned, he briefed us for the mission we're supposed to go on soon. Turns out that a giant drone dropping enemy bombs was found last night at a site next to us. Next to it was a box full of RPG warheads which had been converted to drone bombs, as well as an anti-aircraft missile. In the afternoon, we went out on a mission to destroy Hamas communication antennas and listening devices. Nahman asked me to be Rotem's communicator. It turns out that for the last couple of days, Avishai the communicator had been having a hard time carrying the amplifier on his back, an essential tool, enabling us to increase the reception range of the radios. Kerten from the Eshel team replaced him, but it seemed that Rotem and Kerten didn't get on so well. When Nahman asked me to join the operation command center, I agreed, but I made a point of saying there was no way this would become permanent. "I'm here for my team," I said clearly. Nahman understood me. "Don't worry, Kuno. You're with the team."

We went on the mission. Kerten, Avishai, Rotem and I were together in the operation command center. I think I influenced the operation command, partly because every time we move outside of our site, I insist on high level operational effectiveness –maneuvering, taking cover, and all that. Slowly but surely it had an impact on them. "For a second I couldn't believe my eyes!" Atzitz told me. "The operation command is properly maneuvering and signaling every direction. Kuno, you're making the operation command more efficient, you've got to stay!" I thanked him for the compliment, but repeated the same words I said to Nahman. "Thanks, but no thanks. I'm with the team."

During the mission, we found a stronghold full of pictures of martyrs and Hamas leaders. We went up to its top floor, where the team shot towards the antenna to damage its broadcasting capabilities. On the way, we met the 50th Team, a team from our training course, who are actually part of the supporting company of our battalion but somehow found themselves in our zone. They looked worn out, but it was nice to see and hear from them.

When we returned from the mission, I gathered a few cans of chickpeas from our rations, added a splash of tahini, olive oil, salt, pepper, and cumin, and proudly served everyone hummus. It was absolutely delicious.

We were informed that we would soon get a "refill" – a new supply of food, water, ammunition, and explosives that comes every so often. One of the guys suggested we write letters and send them back with the resupply driver, hoping it would reach our families. Thus we all found ourselves sitting and writing letters. There was something very special about it. Honestly, it was the first time since the war began that I had a chance to write. Suddenly, I started to run over the experiences, events, and thoughts we've gone through so far. It's been so long since I touched a pen. We wrote the letters on pages of a notebook we found here in one of the houses. Everyone sat quietly and wrote. I saw how much it affected the guys. It made us start thinking about home, about our families. I missed Shiran. I wanted to know how she was doing, how she was feeling. Unlike the rest of the team, I was lucky enough to have already spoken with Shiran thanks to the Red Phone, but I was still excited to write to her. I really hoped that she would receive my letter.

Monday, November 6, 2023

The night passed relatively quietly. As always, there was the sound of drones in the sky and Air Force bombings, but nothing out of the ordinary. I was very tired. We didn't sleep much, both because of the night guards shifts and because we'd gotten up relatively early. We were supposed to leave in the morning for a mission, but it was delayed.

I noticed that Meir, Oz, and Omer were writing in a notebook for themselves. I looked at them and remembered the letter from yesterday. It was so fun to write, but beyond that, I'm beginning to understand that we're part of a very significant period for our nation. A period that will be recorded in the pages of history. On a personal level, I'm going through a lot of experiences here that I don't want to forget, and it seems likely that they're going to affect me. I asked the guys if anyone happened to have a spare notebook they weren't using. Meir pulled one out of his bag and gave it to me. From now on, my war will look different. Any free moment I have, I'll try to write and summarize our experiences. This is going to become one of my main pastimes.

At 09:00, Nahman announced that we were leaving. It was a relatively long walk, a movement of 700-meters. This was the first time we've made such a long journey in a built-up area in one go. The bags are on our backs. The sniper team is right behind us, and the rest of the company's teams are moving ahead of us. We are still in Beit Hanoun, but there are slightly fewer signs of destruction on the buildings around us.

We advance slowly, and with all the equipment on me, I can feel myself getting hot and sweaty. There's something very satisfying about a big move. You feel that you are "gaining" serious territory, and at long last our day's progress isn't just confined to three or four lines of houses. We arrived at the site we were supposed to reach:

a five or six-storey building overlooking the sea, and more importantly, overlooking a compound that likely contains a tunnel entrance. We take control of the building and immediately block the entrances. The medical team helps us set up the positions.

After we finish, Rotem, along with all the team commanders, arrives at the "observation dome" over the suspicious compound. We have 2 missions:
1. To destroy the antenna located in the compound.
2. To find the tunnel entrance.

Rotem explains the plan and method of operation to everyone, and we set out for a company-wide mission.

Our team provides covering fire while the rest of the teams scan the compound. I won't go into details, but there's no chance that antenna will work anymore, not after the impressive mortar shots Michaeli sent towards it. We didn't find the tunnel. We were tired, and the longing for home began to weigh on some of the guys. We packed up the site and moved a few dozen meters north, to set up a new stronghold. This time it really was the best stronghold we've had so far. We built ourselves a top-level kitchen, quality bedrooms, and we even had a sitting corner. But the pièce de résistance was the toilets: there were full water heaters on the roof of the house that hadn't been damaged in the bombings, so we could finally use the toilets and the shower. The guys weren't so sure about the shower because we doubted the quality of the water. But to be honest, the prickly heat scared me more.

Generally speaking, there were several significant

accomplishments today for the battalion. We found a tunnel entrance, a Kornet missile, a rocket launcher, and more weaponry. Nahman gave a night briefing. We have intelligence about terrorist groups in the area. We started guard shifts and went to sleep.

During one of the shifts, I was using night vision goggles when suddenly I identified a group of four or five people coming out of a tunnel located south of us. I try to call through the radio to work out if anyone else has identified them besides me. No one answers, and I alert Nahman while keeping an eye on the group. On the one hand, I want to open fire on them, but on the other hand, I want to make sure they aren't our forces. Unfortunately, we've heard about too many friendly fire incidents in this war. I try to initiate communication again when suddenly Atzitz comes on the line "It's us! Don't shoot! We went out on a mission." I'd been so close to opening fire on them. It could have ended in disaster. Turns out they had set out for a mission before my watch, and when I came on watch I wasn't aware of them. I don't know if they sent an update through the radio or not. But when I spotted them, they totally looked like a squad of terrorists. After this small drama, the night passed calmly.

Tuesday, November 7, 2023

Suedi woke me up around 06:30. "Guys," he shouted, "Get up! There's a supply delivery!" I wanted to shut him up so badly. That's really the last thing you want to start your morning with. But it very quickly turned out to be worth it because it was the best supply drop we've had so far. Combat gear, hygiene items, food, underwear, socks, sweets, and – most excitingly – letters! Amitai came to give out the letters, and "Kuno" was written on the top envelope in the pile. I was so excited. Shiran wrote to me that Victor had called when he was evacuated to the hospital and told her all sorts of stories about me. She wrote how much she misses me, that she is strong, and that I shouldn't worry. It was such an emotional and heartening letter. There's no doubt I've got an extraordinary woman by my side.

We went out for various reconnaissance missions. In one of the sites we scanned, the Kesten Team found a white, dusty truck with bloodstains inside. It didn't take much to work out that it had taken part in the October 7th invasion. It was so tangible and shocking. We could feel the evil that was there. I approached the truck and pulled out a Misbaha[14] that was hanging on the vehicle's front mirror. I know it wasn't safe to touch the vehicle, but at that moment, I just wanted to have something to remind me of that event. We waited there while the operations commander came to see the truck. Then, the EITAN, which is in charge of locating missing individuals, arrived to handle the truck, sample the blood and tow it back to Israel. As far as I understand, finding the truck helped establish the death of one of the hostages.

We returned to the stronghold with "spoils" of rice, lentils, oil, and more. Until now, every time we've had a moment to rest, I've cooked food for the team, but Meir and

---

14 Muslim prayer beads.

Suedi also decided to step up their cooking game. I finally had some time to write.

Nahman gave a night briefing. At around midnight, we'll go out for an ambush at the site where the truck was found. We speculated that because we'd found the truck and had been in the area, terrorists would try to come during the night. At sites near the truck, we found food and coffee cups that seemed to have been used just recently. We finished the briefing and went to sleep.

Victor came back! After a few days of not being with us they brought him back along with the supplies. Honestly, I missed him.

One of the significant challenges in this war is that it doesn't look like a war. There's a misconception that in war you're constantly fighting, leaping and jumping between alleys while shooting and engaging in intense combat, with a face full of soot and bloodstained hands. But during most of the fighting, you don't actually encounter terrorists. There are moments of quiet and tranquility, as well as many moments when you sit bored inside a building not knowing what to do with yourself. There are moments when everything around you feels like virtual reality. Hundreds of destroyed buildings, giant craters formed by bombings. A lot of noise. One of the big difficulties in all this is trying to stay alert and ready all the time. When you have visuals on a terrorist, it's very easy to be ready to engage. It's your basic instinct. But Hamas fighters don't fight like fighters, they fight like mice from their burrows. Occasionally they pop their heads out, shoot, and run back in. Most of our war against them is actually against explosives and booby-trapped areas, and as a combat soldier, it's very hard to maintain vigilance when you barely face the enemy. I realized very quickly that our challenge in this battle wouldn't only be in daring combat and impressive acts of bravery, but rather the opposite: the quiet routines of fighters who manage to remain calm and adhere to our guidelines and procedures. Those who don't give up on all those minute and irritating details – are the ones who will win the war.

Wednesday, November 8, 2023

At 00:30 Nahman wakes us up for the ambush. Just before leaving, I give out caffeine pills to the guys. The ambush went relatively smoothly. Every so often we heard strange noises. Thanks to the caffeine pills, I stayed completely alert. When we returned in the middle of the night, Amitai said that someone shot a missile at them. We told him disbelievingly that while it was probably a serious explosion, he was exaggerating a bit. "I'm telling you," he insisted. "The whole building shook, there's no way it was something minor."

When we woke up the next morning, to our surprise, we found a shell in our staircase. A shell! We could see the hole it made in the wall. It was a real miracle that no one was hurt. The sniper team was on the roof, our team on the floor below, and the Atzitz team beneath us. If the shell had hit any other point in the building, we likely would have spent last night busy evacuating casualties or worse. It turns out it was actually a misfire by the artillery unit who shot towards us and miscalculated the ranges. Crazy! You can be the best soldier in the army and still die because of idiots around you.

I look out the window and see fog outside. Not much time has passed when suddenly, the radio reports that there are 18 terrorists emerging from tunnels in our zone and running south. "Guys, get ready! We're going after the terrorists," Nahman commands. During the night, the brigade had made sure to fill some of the tunnel entrances with explosives, which is probably why those terrorists were fleeing.

We prepare to go out for a company-wide pursuit, but it takes us too long. Let's just say that if someone tried to escape the area, they likely succeeded. In any case, we perform combat procedures, form an exit strategy, and head out for the chase. There's no structured plan, just advancing southward in the hope of finding terrorists trying to escape and take them down. After 4 hours of pursuit and scanning dozens of sites, we stop and Nahman spots a half-burnt white truck on the side of the road. We approach the truck and discover hand grenades, ammunition, vests, and a map inside.

All this time there are a lot of gunshots in the area. We enter a nearby stronghold and make sure no one approaches the truck until the EITAN (missing persons) team arrives. It takes time. A lot of time. We are already exhausted. We're desperate to get out of there and return to the stronghold. We didn't bring enough food or water with us, and the guys started to dehydrate. Lahad, the logistics officer, goes out with a few representatives from the team to bring food and water from our stronghold. We were absolutely worn out from fatigue. Rotem, in communication with the brigade, decided that there's no reason to wait for the EITAN team and approached the truck. He took out all the grenades, and Yemini, Nahman, and I blew them up with explosives while the guys tried to decipher the map in the stronghold.

Rotem started to dismantle the vehicle and to try to start the engine. I personally thought that was very dangerous and irresponsible. Who knew there weren't any remains or DNA samples of hostages whose identification he was obscuring? Besides, who said the vehicle wasn't booby-trapped? But Rotem was determined, and when he couldn't get it started, he tried to dismantle the ignition. That was too much for me. I told him I was leaving and I went back to the stronghold with Yemini.

We were told to wait in the stronghold until the D9 arrived to tow the vehicle. All the officers left for various reasons. Time passed. We thought we'd wait there for twenty minutes, but an hour had already gone by. Then two hours. It's only us and the company's sniper team left. Time continued to pass and we still couldn't get in touch with them. It really started to annoy me. I told the guys that if the officers didn't respond soon, we had to head back to the stronghold. The sun was about to set, we didn't have a "switchblade" (a location response device that allows other forces to know where we are in real-time) and we were on the outskirts of our zone. Everything is clear in the light of day, but at night we could find ourselves in the midst of a friendly fire disaster in a short space of time.

Rotem comes on the line: "Guys, don't move anywhere! The Dubi (D9) will be there in a second!" I try to explain the situation over the radio, but he doesn't respond. So, another twenty minutes pass, and the sun is about to set. I want us to rush back to the stronghold, and most of the team agrees with me, but Victor declares, "Guys, I'm not disobeying an order, you can go but I'm staying here." That completely infuriated me. What kind of statement is that, we obviously aren't going to leave anyone in the field! And it's obvious that we're not going to start dragging him out by force. There was a disgusting feeling in the air. A mixture of nerves, fear, anger, and frustration. A bit of everything at once. Fancy that, Nahman isn't there for one moment, and everything here becomes one big mess.

Suddenly Rotem appeared with a few guys from the Kesten Team. He has a battery and is trying to start the vehicle. When I ask Avishai, the communicator, if they have a "switchblade," he says no because Rotem forgot it at the stronghold. Incensed, I say to the guys, "Yalla. Let's go." We do a roll call, and I start moving towards the stronghold. It had been one of the hardest days of the war so far. I felt like it really damaged my trust in Rotem's decision-making ability.

We returned to the stronghold angry and fuming, but very quickly we had a team talk about the event and ended the day well. We made dinner and listen to Nahman's briefing.

At night, we were informed that we're leaving for a 48-hour refresh, although personally, I didn't believe it would happen. Anyway, at 23:00, we woke up and started packing our gear and getting ourselves ready to leave Gaza. There was excitement in the air, leaving after 11 days of fighting. A moment before we loaded our bags up on the vehicles to leave, we were informed that we were staying. Due to several intelligence findings, the Chief of the Southern Command decided to pause exits and to change missions. I wasn't surprised; even as I was packing my bag I had a feeling we'd stay, but still, it affected me. The longing for family and for Shiran, for a hug from her that I missed so badly.

We returned the bags to their place and continued with guard shifts. Meir and I talked about the great privilege that we have of serving, the understanding that it's difficult for everyone, and how we can't judge anyone. We took a deep breath in anticipation of another long day.

Thursday, November 9, 2023

In the morning, we woke up with a strange feeling. I tried using the Red Phone to reach Shiran. Amir, Shiran's commander, answered and said, "Shiran isn't on base, she went to her grandmother's funeral." Shock, disbelief. It took me 2-3 minutes to digest, and then I burst into tears. After 7 minutes of crying, I gathered the team. I told them about Shiran's grandmother and her unique character, and we agreed as a team to try to be more giving, to compensate for the loss of her grandmother. During our conversation on the Red Phone, Amir called Shiran on his mobile and let me speak to her. "I'm sorry Elkana, I didn't want you to know," she said. I didn't know how to convey to her what I was feeling at that moment. "My love," I said, "know that I love you, and everything is fine. I've had a bit of time to process it because we continued our combat routine immediately after I heard. But if we have to face such difficulty, then I'm glad that the team is here with me – it's a great source of strength."

I truly feel that we are a significant part of the war. Not just because of the physical combat with terrorists, but also because we keep coming across things related to the hostages. Today we found a child's vest stained with blood and a toy Torah. It's impossible to put into words the emotions that run through you at the sight of such things.

One of the things that shocked me in Beit Hanoun – which really shocked me – was that the vast majority of houses we passed through had Hamas uniforms, weapons, explosives, or combat gear. Almost without exception, we find a picture of a martyr at the entrance to the house. We found explosives and terror infrastructure inside schools and hospitals, but what shocked me more than anything was the fact that they use children's beds to hide grenades, weapons, and all types of combat equipment. Even if I thought their war was justified, I would never put a grenade under my child's bed. I can't understand how a father and mother of a young child could place an explosive device under their bed. It just sickens me.

And even more infuriating – the buildings belonging to

UNRWA that we went through were also full of explosives and combat equipment.

We had a conversation with the battalion commander in the Atzitz team's stronghold. We talked about how we need to understand what's happening and which tasks lie ahead of us. After the conversation, we moved to a new stronghold, relatively close to us. There was no gas or stove there, and frankly it was less good than the previous site in general. Meir, Kaneti, and I went back to the old stronghold to retrieve the stove and gas, and after an hour of work, the stronghold was as it should be.

When we finished setting it up, nine of us went to search the Hamas compound. We went through dozens of buildings and apartments, and in each one, we moved wardrobes, lifted mattresses, removed bedding, and made sure there were no terrorists left on site. We also found important intelligence materials, like the camera of a Gazan journalist with footage of Hamas operatives training for the attack on October 7th. I saw a video in which ten Hamas members were driving a pick-up truck with guns slung over their shoulders, and the whole street was cheering and encouraging them. At one point, it became very difficult for me. The mission began at noon and ended at night; I felt exhausted and fatigue took over me. I felt sick. When we returned, we were very tired, but thank God there was a good ratio for guard duty, of 1:7, so each shift lasted just half an hour, allowing for good rest. I felt like it really saved me.

Friday, November 10, 2023

It's a moment before the start of Shabbat and I can't comprehend that another Shabbat is passing by. Time here has its own rules. It goes both fast and slow simultaneously.

In the middle of the night, those who weren't part of yesterday's mission were woken up for an ambush. Truth be told, I felt a bit sorry for them: they got up for the ambush at 03:00; it's now 15:23, and they still haven't returned. We heard over the radio that they captured a lot of weapons, snipers, and RPGs. We rested well, organized the house we were in, and went for two supermarket "runs" to get supplies: oil, salt, and some chocolate and snacks. We ate and it was really nice.

At 15:45 the team was just returning from the ambush. They found a lot of rifles, grenades, ammunition and IEDs. It turned out that there was almost a friendly fire incident, but thank God it was avoided. During the day, there was a very loud explosion – the whole building shook, and the blast was very strong. Every time we entered a building, we covered the doors and openings with blankets so we couldn't be seen. Everything went flying in the explosion, and to tell you the truth my ears have been hurting a lot since then. But apart from that, I'm fine. I think a lot about Shiran and how I wish I could be by her side in these hard moments. I think a lot about our dear grandmother, and I'm glad I had the great privilege of knowing her, but on the other hand, I can't let these thoughts overwhelm me; I need to focus on the war.

Meir and Suedi prepared lunch for the guys with rice, lentils, and hummus. It turned out tasty.

My hand is already hurting from writing, and I also need to start getting the equipment ready for the evening. I might manage to write a little more before Shabbat.

Saturday Night, November 11, 2023

I didn't manage to write as I had hoped before Shabbat started. Shabbat came in faster than expected. I was busy with the preparations for the stronghold.

It was a very emotional Kabbalat Shabbat.[15] We went up to the Atzitz team's apartment and sang the Shabbat prayers together. It seems Michaeli took photos, so we might have a memento of it. Nahman and Atzitz gave a Dvar Torah,[16] and I added a few words about our dear grandmother. I can't seem to get thoughts about Grandma out of my head. It's hard for me not to be with the family at this time. I want to be with Shiran.

In the morning, we understood from the brigade's situational assessment that a difficult event occurred yesterday, just a few hundred meters away from us. Four soldiers were killed, and another six were severely injured at a booby-trapped entrance of a mosque. Every time we hear about a soldier being killed it's painful and heartbreaking, especially when it's people as special as Moshe Yedidyah Leiter, Sergey Shmarkin, Matan Meir, and Yossi Hershkovitz. I think about all those who have fallen and will fall in this

---

15 Friday evening Shabbat prayers which "welcome" the Sabbath.
16 Literally "a word of Torah", a short religious sermon.

campaign. Each one was an entire world. Each has a family. I hope all this won't be in vain. It must not be in vain. There is no doubt that this news affected us. This event made me much more alert and suspicious of anything strange.

We followed the prayer with Kiddush,[17] said "HaMotzi"[18] for the challah, and returned to the apartment. We sang together with the whole team. We went to sleep and woke up to a "resupply." There were trays with schnitzels, fruit platters, and cakes that our friends Bashi, Abayof, and Hamo sent us. In the morning, we said Kiddush and went to search for various terror sites southeast of us. We made bets on when we would return to the shelter. Everyone made a bet. I said 17:40.

There's something very tiring in these searches, it's hard to maintain discipline and fundamental combat routines and habits. But I keep telling myself that this is what will save me and the team: to keep proper distance, maintain eye contact, constantly look for threats, kneel or lie down during stops, and scan every site for people and explosives.

During the searches, we need to look in all the closets and under all the furniture, while keeping cover, not removing protective gear. In short, there are many things to remember and do.

We continued the searches and found a house with two EFP (explosively formed penetrator) charges, an APL (anti-personnel landmine), and two additional spray charges.[19]

---

17 Traditional blessing over wine which commences each Shabbat meal.
18 The traditional blessing recited before eating bread.
19 These are all various anti-personnel bombs.

There were lots of maps of the Gaza Envelope,[20] a first aid kit bag, electric remote bomb detonators, and tons of intelligence materials, phones, and work permits for Israel. It turns out that the son of the apartment owner was a suicide bomber. We continued the searches until 15:00 and found all sorts of combat equipment. We returned to the shelter at 15:40. Shlomi won the bet!

We arranged the equipment and had another evening of singing. Lately, discipline within the team has been a bit lax, and it's hard to maintain it. We sing relatively loudly during our searches, which could expose our location. But on the other hand, it gives us a bit of sanity and routine as the war continues.

Shabbat finished. We made Havdallah and a procedural briefing for the night. Afterwards, a post-Shabbat cigarette. I smoke occasionally for the atmosphere, or as Michaeli says, "pure escapism." We arranged the equipment again and got ready for sleep. I'm taking advantage of this time to write. Just before going to sleep, the battalion commander comes to talk to us; it seems like everyone understands the importance of talking to the guys, of trying to maintain an operational atmosphere. To remind us for what and why we are fighting. It's hard for all of us; we want to go home to relax, see our wives and families. The battalion commander updates us on the IDF's situation. It's a moment of pride. The IDF already surrounds Gaza from every direction, and now they are starting to take control of the Shifa Hospital.

---

20 The populated areas in the Southern District of Israel that are within 4.3 miles of the Gaza Strip border, and which bore the brunt of the October 7 attacks.

Our commanding officer tells us that our next mission is to fight alongside the 98th Division and take control of Khan Yunis. The guys are a bit anxious, but in my opinion, it's no different than the anxiety we felt three weeks ago in the Sevivon neighborhood of Beit Hanoun. The conversation ends, and we go to sleep.

At 23:24, I continue writing between guard shifts before I drift off. There are very loud explosions from the Air Force tonight; I'm interested to know where they are bombing. We'll know tomorrow, although it feels relatively close. With every explosion, our stronghold trembles. I'm going back to sleep, good night.

At 23:45, a message on the radio: "Get everyone ready to gear up. At 00:30, the trucks will be here to pick us up from the battalion stronghold."

Sunday, November 12, 2023

At 00:15 they wake up the whole team. I tell them as a joke that we're heading to Khan Yunis, and the guys have no clue what's going on. Nahman gathers everyone and announces that we're going out for a refresh. Excitement to the max. We pack our equipment and head out on foot towards the battalion stronghold. It's been two weeks since we were there, and it's crazy to see the change. There were all sorts of houses which posed threats to the stronghold, and today none of them remained. We arrive at the shelter and wait for the transport to pick us up. When we get to the convoy, the drivers tell us that the IDF has already reached Gaza City and has made serious advances. There is something very encouraging about it. It gives the soldiers a burst of confidence that they are not being sent into the zone like sheep to slaughter but that there are clear operational goals. The atmosphere is good; everyone is singing songs and clapping; we're crossing the border and heading straight to Bror Hayil. A barbecue is waiting for us there, along with music – pure enjoyment! We organize the equipment. Before that, I managed to speak with Shiran and send a message to my mom. There's no-one like my Shiran. It's great to hear that she is strong; it fills me with pride. We finish organizing the equipment and get on the buses for the journey to Ashkelon.

We arrive in Ashkelon, where we pass from station to station. We make sure all the equipment is in order, clean, and ready for use for the next outing. I won't elaborate too much; I'll just say that I really missed home, Shiran and the family.

Monday, November 13, 2023

Today we're heading home, and I'm filled with mixed feelings. A combination of great joy and gratitude to God that we are all healthy and whole, along with a feeling of being finished but not completely satisfied. I went to pick up Shiran from the base, and from there we went straight to a restaurant in Herzliya where we like to sit. There's something special and meaningful about the two of us being in the military. I feel that it is a great privilege. I was glad that I managed to go to Grandma's shiva[21] and be with the family.

Two days after I left, we woke up to a sad morning. We heard the terrible news about Yedidya Asher Lev who fell in battle. Yedidya was a soldier of mine when I commanded a team in Officer School. I first met him as a quiet and reserved guy, but as I got to know him, I realized just how great he was. Yedidya was truly a special character in my life. He was a man of humility, who cared for everyone around him, and who did everything in his characteristic quietness. He didn't speak much, but when he did, it was always full of insight and depth. Along with his quiet nature, Yedidya was very knowledgeable and I loved talking with him. I felt I had a lot to learn from him. People like him, even when they think differently than you, still know how to listen and show respect. He transmitted strength to me, and I always loved seeing his mischievous smile.

He was one of the first to volunteer for any annoying task, and despite not talking much about family, I sensed that he was a very warm and family-oriented man. After I heard about his death, I found a video his family had sent me during one of the times I wanted to cheer up the soldiers after we'd spent a long time on base. It was on the eve of Rosh Hashanah, and his family sent me a video greeting for the holiday. Hearing his sister in the video saying "Yedidushkila" gave me chills. I felt that he was embraced by his family's

---

21 A week-long mourning period after the funeral.

love. I was so upset that I couldn't visit during the shiva, and asked the rest of my team to send me photos from the short period in which I had the honor of commanding Yedidya so we could pass them on to his parents.

Although the time was accompanied by difficult and painful events, I tried to detach myself and be with Shiran and the family. Those three days with them were amazing, and we'd waited for them for so long. It was really a breath of fresh air.

Second Notebook

Beit Lahiya, Al-Attara

It's Sunday and I'm writing for the first time since leaving Gaza. The winds are so strong that I can barely write in the notebook.

Thursday, November 16, 2023

In the morning, we returned from our "refresher," and the platoon split up into various training sessions: demolition, camouflage, navigation, first aid, and more. I was in demolition training. Strange to admit, but it was fun to return to the army, and the demolition training was important. I went over things I had already managed to forget, even though we dealt with demolition a lot in Gaza. We returned in the evening to the countryside in Kfar Bilu. We organized equipment, then had dinner and went to sleep.

Friday, November 17, 2023

Most of the team woke up in the morning for physical training, and I took Oz and Omer to continue the demolition training at the Adam facility. I felt that the training on Friday was a bit less relevant for me, so I took the time to visit family. I drove to Modi'in and visited my uncle and aunt, Dror and Elisheva, and their kids Yankele and Ayelet. By chance I also spent some time with my grandparents there, and it was emotional to see everyone. I then visited Shiran on base, and together we went to visit my brother, Or. It was special for the three of us to be in the same place. Afterward,

Shiran and I returned to the car, talked a bit, recited Psalms together, hugged, kissed, and said goodbye.

No one compares to my Shiranush. During the war, I discovered how many phenomenal character traits she has. She is so sensitive and caring towards everyone around her, innocent and full of faith. She loves me very much. From time to time, she sends me messages like "Elkana, remember to judge people favorably," or "Try not to get upset," or "It's hard for me to not gossip, but I really try." In short, without a doubt, I have been truly blessed.

I drove back towards Kfar Bilu, and on the way, I got into an accident, which was honestly partly my fault. An inattentive driver almost crashed into me, and when I swerved, I hit a car beside me. I didn't have time to stop. We quickly pulled over, exchanged information, and I continued driving, not dwelling too much on the strange pain in my back. On the way, I also stopped in Na'an to see Racheli – she's amazing. Recently, she hasn't stopped worrying about us and treating us. I spent some time with Racheli, Nadav, and Lula (Ella), and they loaded the car with all sorts of treats for everyone. We arrived back at Kfar Bilu and started preparing for Shabbat. We understood that this would be the last night before the incursion. I spoke with Shiran and sent a message to the family group chat that we would be switching off our phones soon. I didn't have time to pray the evening Shabbat prayers. I was busy preparing the equipment for combat.

Afterward, we had Shabbat dinner with the company, and after the meal, I went to shower at a family friend's house in Kfar Bilu before going to sleep.

Shabbat, November 18, 2023

2nd Outing

On Shabbat morning, we woke up for final preparations. We boarded the bus, removed unnecessary items, filled up water bottles, and headed towards the power station in Ashkelon, and made final preparations again. I checked every aspect of my equipment, including shoes, uniform, weapons, vest, helmet, knee pads, and a backpack weighing 45 kilograms alone. It turned out that I, weighing 75 kilograms, was carrying 60 kilograms.

After turning off our phones, Rotem gathered us for a company talk. In the previous round of fighting, I had a hard time with Rotem. I felt like I couldn't trust him because of some of the decisions he had made, so it was difficult for me to think about another round of combat under his command. But, truth be told, he surprised me several times during the conversation. I saw that he was struggling. He talked about having made some mistakes but having learned from them after the last round, and being pleased that we had given him feedback. I think that saying what he said wasn't a given, and even though I had previous difficulties with him, I said to all the team members, "Guys, don't give up on him. Let's give him another chance." I really appreciated the conversation. It couldn't have been easy to stand in his place, and he did it with a full heart and without grudges because he truly wanted us to improve as soldiers.

Encouraged by the conversation with Rotem, we ate the

Shabbat meal and headed out with the Humvees towards Gaza.

There was a lot of dust in the air, some concerns about how the current round of combat would look, but also a lot of strength and pride. We crossed the border. Gaza was full of Israeli flags. We drove and saw the first sunset on the sands of Gaza. It was crazy to see the number of vehicles, tanks, trucks, and armored personnel carriers, all with flags. We entered 5 kilometers into Gaza, to the brigade stronghold. We understand that we are participating in a very significant mission, which, at its end, holds the possibility of rescuing the hostages. It's amazing how within a few hours, we transform from pampered family members at home to soldiers one hundred percent focused on the most important mission possible. It's clear to all of us that we will do everything in our power to execute this mission to the best of our abilities.

We are supposed to open an axis that is two kilometers long, to allow the Shayetet[22] and commando forces to pass through for a hostage rescue operation.

Night fell and I heard a team in the distance performing the Havdallah ceremony. I joined them from a distance and responded with "Amen." We moved locations inside the stronghold and prepared to go to sleep. I woke up for the first radio shift. I saw that the guys were thirsty and a little hungry, so I approached the armored personnel carrier, the "Puma," that was in the area and asked them for some water and snacks. I returned with all the goods.

---

22 An elite commando unit, similar to the Navy SEALs.

As if I were in a market, I called out offering the items, and threw them to each person. The atmosphere immediately improved.

We went to sleep, but it was freezing. We realized that the cold would play a significant role in the upcoming weeks of combat. Luckily, I brought a GORE-TEX sleeping bag with me, which helped me keep warm at night.

Sunday, November 19, 2023

1:00: Beginning of our maneuver, Beit Lahiya. Bone-chilling cold. We all shiver, but you quickly warm up when you walk with all the gear and weight on your back. We move in pairs, and every few meters the force stops, kneels for a moment, and then continues the maneuver, leaving the battalion's operational area.

Our progress is telescopic, meaning it's relatively fast but in a single line. We aim to quickly reach multiple control points in order to facilitate movement on the axis. This is complex because we are entering deep into enemy territory, but the surrounding area is not yet cleared of terrorists. Additionally, to our south are located Nahal Brigade forces, increasing the risk of friendly fire when identifying terrorists from the south.

We start moving quietly, passing by a fuel station and greenhouses, identifying a faint beeping in the background. There's concern about an explosive device, but we don't want to approach and delay. We continue moving forward.

We advance almost as far as the school and stop at an orchard north of it. We wait to continue moving forward. It's pitch black; I have night-vision goggles, but they're broken. I see two images rather than one clear one, which makes me dizzy; so, sometimes I look with only one eye. We continue the movement. We are on a ridge line, with the "bathtub" area below us – meaning a destruction zone in low ground which we can easily observe from the area that surrounds it – and the sites that we are supposed to take over.

The Kesten team took over their building to fit the rest of the company in for combat. We stop on site for about 30-45 minutes. It's freezing. According to the intelligence we have, we are close to an ambush and a tunnel entrance, so we try to stay alert.

We move towards our target, smelling once again the putrid odor of carcasses. We pass by an animal pen. We begin to occupy and clear our building. Squads A and B remove their packs and clear the building. We, Squad C, entered afterwards with our bags. We are a bit drained, but once the sun rises, it's easy to stay awake. Nahman gives instructions, and we start sleeping and taking guard shifts. Around 15:00, we wake up for the upcoming mission of expanding the southern defense line. We move 100 meters to the southeast.

We enter the site. The place is filled with electric wires and cables. We cut everything and clear the building. The building stinks. In general, this area is very poor compared to Beit Hanoun. Houses are abandoned. There's usually an animal pen, stable, or hen house on the first floor, and the living quarters are on the second floor. The houses are empty of equipment. We entered the building and, after finishing the search, set up a defense for a team that went to clear another area. At the end of our search, we identify a ladder connecting our site to a nearby site slightly northward, and decide to detonate the site. Rain begins to fall. Nahman goes out with the charge, loads explosives on the entry door, and throws two more demolition blocks into the building through the window.

We count backwards, and then a **massive** explosion.

The entire building collapses, likely because it was rigged with explosives or filled with gas canisters. Anyway, Rotem decides that it's too dangerous a site to scan. It was decided that we would return to our stronghold. Kashi, Yemini, and I start making our way towards our outpost when suddenly, 20 meters from us, there's a strong explosion. It turns out the convoy confused their coordinates and crossed our stronghold's defense line, detonating an explosive near us. When we returned to our outpost, Shlomi and Amitai informed us that these idiots also shot a Matador at us (an advanced shoulder-mounted rocket). The friendly fire issue here is no joke. It was truly dangerous. We get orginazed for the night and prepare the stronghold. We throw some more blankets on the windows, making sure everything is dark. Nahman gives a night-time briefing. We have two guard positions. The sniper team left for a better position with another team.

We start guarding in half-hour shifts. At 23:00, I take the third shift with Yemini and hear a report that the "resupply" is arriving. Yemini and I decide to wait a bit before waking up the crew since we've understood how it works – first they announce it on the radio and then they drag it out for some half hour. When we understand the supplies are indeed coming, we wake everyone up. The time is 23:58. At around 01:40, the crew returns from the resupply. I "steal" a sandwich and some pickles and go to sleep.

At 03:00, Suedi wakes us up. "The Spear and Squad B are heading out on the mission, we need one more volunteer from Squad C." I volunteer. Rain starts to fall. We climb over IDF barriers. I take Victor's night vision goggles, because mine is in worse shape. There are nine of us. The ground is muddy, and I feel the mud sticking to my boots, making them heavier. We pass a lettuce field and head towards our target. The Spear leads and moves towards a destroyed building blown up by the Air Force. Omer, Shlomi, Amitai, and I enter a nearby building and take cover while maintaining visual contact with the remote control center and part of the team. Suedi and Nahman go together, and Suedi launches a LAW (light anti-armor weapon) in the direction of a suspicious building. Immediately after the bang, Michaeli fires a few explosive grenades towards the building. Michaeli's a legend, it's exciting to see the impact of his shots.

As we leave, we receive information about an enemy ambush composed of five terrorists – a bomber-setter, an RPG gunner, a sniper, and two fighters with Kalashnikovs. We didn't encounter any of them, but I really hope that we neutralized them inside the building. I do know that right before Michaeli sent a barrage, a light was flashing at the site, but after his barrage, it became pitch-black.

We retreat, and a light drizzle of rain begins to fall. What a relief that the rain waited until now. Being outside when it's raining can be awful.

On the way back to the stronghold, we passed by the building that was detonated in the afternoon and thank God that everything went safely. I quietly recited a blessing, "Blessed be He who performed a miracle for me in this place." We enter the outpost, and I immediately take off the vest, the night vision goggles, and my uniform. I was boiling hot. We conduct a thorough assessment. Nahman needs to go to Eshel's outpost for an officers' meeting. Oz and I gear up, escort him, and return to the post. We scarf down some food and go to sleep.

Monday, November 20, 2023

06:00 – Meir wakes me up in the morning, "Kuno, get up for guard duty." The truth is, I feel like I slept well. I'm pretty sure that they skipped one of my shifts, and now I'm the only one at the post. In the background, it's quiet, and occasionally we hear gunfire and explosions. Liam, the communications deputy company commander, slept with us at the site and left the communication device on the battalion command channel near the radio post. I love that. You understand what's going on in the area.

Suddenly, there's a lot of shooting and reports over the radio. A mortar explodes relatively close to us. I can't see where it fell, but chunks of concrete and dust fly toward us.

I sit next to the radio post and write. It's become a hobby for me lately. The guards change around me. Amitai, then Shlomi, followed by Suedi, and now Oz. It's nice to write in real-time. It's hard to keep up with the pace of events here. Anyway, I'm going to take a break now to pray, eat, and sleep. It's currently 10:00. Good morning.

P.S: Dear Shiranush, I miss you! Hopefully, I'll manage to reach the Red Phone today and give you a call.

I managed to sleep a little. At 11:15, Meir wakes us up. Apparently, they briefed moments ago about further commands. There are rumors that our site is one of the smelliest, but it seems like we've gotten used to it because the smell is relatively okay to me. Every time we come back from a mission I rediscover the foul smell, but within 5 minutes, I'm used to it again. Victor informs us that at 12:30, we are heading for a mission at the school. Apparently, the auxiliary company eliminated a terrorist there yesterday, and today they identified three more terrorists. Before we leave, we organize the post and clean up another room for gear, numbering the walls from 1 to 15 to mark where each person places their gear. I am #6.

Nahman begins a briefing. Three minutes into the briefing, someone communicates to Nahman over the radio, "Change of mission." We take Nahman to an officers' meeting to receive new commands. I take advantage of the time to sleep a bit. Nahman returns from the meeting and tells the Spear Squad, me and Yemini to be ready. We head out before the others to set up two breaches in the buildings we are going to take over. We plan to execute a company-wide capture of a new facility located to the south of our stronghold. The plan is to detonate four breaches simultaneously and then clear the areas. Honestly, if there's anyone in the team I want to do these detonations with, it's Yemini. The guy is extremely professional. I've been lucky to be his partner, even if he drives me crazy sometimes.

Yemini and I prepare a remote breach frame and approach the building with our charges. I give Yemini a look and count backwards. 3... 2... 1... Yemini triggers the detonator... **a strong blast!** We finish detonating all the charges and begin the mission. I wait expectantly behind cover to see if our charge was effective. Yosifon checks and says "it worked, it worked," with a big smile on his face. He tells me, "Kuno, you've given them a King's Passageway."

We start the invasion. I am with the Spear Squad advancing towards our structure, all the while glancing back towards the wall that we blew up. Wow, I'm filled with pride. Our IED worked very well, but when we entered the site which was supposed to become our new guard post, I was dumbfounded. Total chaos. Insane destruction. It's all dust and stones, absolutely suffocating in here, and this is supposed to be our new guard post... But an hour of cleanup did its job; it seems we managed to tame the mess.

We are going to sleep, and I am making use of the time to write. The time now is 19:20 and we were just informed a few minutes ago that we need to be ready for a company-wide departure at 21:00. In the background, I hear gunfire again, but it has long become routine. I get into bed, if one can call it that – the stinky, torn, dusty mattress we found in one of the rooms.

20:17 – Suddenly, a massive explosion, the whole building shakes. I ask, somewhat indifferent, if anyone knows what's going on, but no one answers me. People no longer get worked up about explosions anymore. Someone next to me mumbles in their sleep, "Our building probably got hit by a missile," and goes back to sleep. I try to doze off but can't, a little anxious about the mission tonight. I have a feeling something interesting will happen there.

22:15 – Victor wakes us up; I get myself organized and fill my vest with a few more protein bars and Mentos, and then they inform us that the mission seems to be postponed.

Turns out there was another catastrophic event in the battalion today and it was only by some miracle that it didn't end in a crazy disaster wiping out an entire team. One of the companies in the battalion guided a combat helicopter to a site full of terrorists.The only thing they didn't know was that at the same time, a team from another company started to enter that same structure in order to eliminate those terrorists.

The helicopter was instructed by the company commander to fire two missiles at the building, which, miraculously, were duds and did not explode. One of the soldiers was severely injured as a result of the helicopter's shooting, but there's no doubt that it could have ended much worse. I won't go into the details, but commanders definitely need to be more careful in their firing. I really hope that we at least learn from this event which was nearly catastrophic. And I especially hope that the injured soldier will recover and heal.

I heard this horrible story and went back to sleep.

Tuesday, November 21, 2023

In the morning, Victor wakes us up. "Come on, guys, in 10 minutes we're heading to the school."

It's relatively cold, but very quickly I realize it's a battalion-wide operation, and that we are involved in the main part of the mission. Tanks, D9 bulldozers, combat soldiers, Air Force. All working together. Slowly, all forces start positioning themselves in the groves that surround the school, and prepare for the attack.

Our team takes cover. We received intelligence about a tunnel opening close to us, and the D9 near us starts to clear everything in the vicinity of the school. After a few minutes of work, it breaks down a structure made of tin, and we see a tunnel opening. We take over the school, each team clearing a floor. We are left to rest in the classrooms for further instructions. I sleep a little, then use the opportunity to call Shiran on the Red Phone. I heard in her voice that she was a bit stressed. I asked what's wrong, and Shiran told me that she's very worried about me. I reiterated the usual mantra: everything is fine, you have nothing to worry about. I am a highly professional fighter, I am cautious and alert and pay attention to everything happening around me. "But Elkana," she said, "what difference does it make that you are so professional and careful when yesterday there was a friendly fire incident in the battalion? Are you aware that a combat helicopter fired on your team? It doesn't matter how professional you are. You are not immune to the mistakes of others." I tried to reassure her that I am the great-grandson of Grandma Mally who survived the

Holocaust with unbelievable stories, the kind where she always prevailed no matter the situation. We finished the conversation, and just before I hung up, I asked Shiran to send flowers to Amitai's wife and to send regards to the wives of all the team members.

Shaked asked me to carry the Negev (a light machine gun) so he could carry more equipment. So after a very long time, I once again became the Spear Team's "Negevist." It was nice to walk at the head of the initiating team. We arrive at the new site, and as we start to approach it, there's a horrible smell of carcasses. I scan the building and discover the carcass of an enormous cow at the entrance to the building. Thousands of giant bluebottle flies. Truly revolting. I try to see if there is another entrance to the building and survey the building together with Nahman and again – another cow carcass. We won't be here much longer.

We are sitting next to the building, waiting to understand where we go from here. Kaneti starts telling all kinds of stories about the girls he met on his trip to Colombia and Mexico, and after 40 minutes, we head to another stronghold.

Victor, Kashi, and Meir prepared a luxurious dinner that included rice, smoked tuna, and various fruits they picked from the orchard nearby. I ate and then simply collapsed on the floor. Finally, after four days of fighting, we managed to properly utilize the stronghold. It seems like it's going to be a good night, as the guard duty rotation ratio is really good. Earlier, there was a battalion-wide situational assessment, and they informed us that apparently in the coming days, we'll be entering Jabaliya. Until then, let's hope for some normal sleep.

Wednesday, November 22, 2023

04:40 – So far, I've only stood guard twice. Our current stronghold has a significant advantage as it's close to the logistic axis, meaning supplies were really close to us. We received cheese, pastrami, a lot of tasty protein snacks, sweet drinks, plenty of dried fruits, and what I consider the real winnings of the war – dried meat.

The logistic axis, although close, was still tough to reach, especially when transporting supplies. According to my estimation, the backpack that I carried around weighed roughly 65 kilos. The moment I put it on my back, the sack pushed my helmet forward, covering my eyes and I could barely see, so I asked Suedi to guide me.

There are moments when my hand hurts from writing and I can't wait to finish. But there are moments like now when I really enjoy writing. It passes the time and helps me process the experiences that we are going through here. I think this is the kind of book my children will enjoy reading. They will say, "My dad wrote this," "He really was there and fought." My guard duty will end soon, and I'll wake up Michaeli to replace me. After that, I'll go back to sleep. This night, with many hours of sleep, came at the perfect time.

08:45 – I woke up, and most of the team was already awake. We feel like we slept well last night. I fell asleep during my first shift last night, and Suedi woke me up. From my perspective, that's a very serious incident. Although I wasn't in the most critical guard position, the point is that I didn't do my duty. It could have been a matter of life and death for me and my comrades. And I would have never forgiven myself if anything happened to them. This happened because I was extremely tired and sat down on a chair. Such irresponsibility on my part. It's important for me that I have a conversation today with the team about this incident to raise awareness about how easy it is for us to "break guard duty" and what it could lead to.

I said the morning prayers, prepared myself a toast with cheese from the resupply and ketchup from the army rations on a skillet with olive oil. After the morning check-in, I cleaned the clogged toilets that had already run out of water. Wow, that was disgusting. I asked Kaneti, our medic, for a glove, pushed my hand into the toilet, cleared out the wipes, poured in water and soap, and started scrubbing. By the end of it, the bathrooms were clean. I washed my hands with some hand sanitizer, and went to treat my feet. Terrible fungus. I wiped my feet, applied an antifungal cream, and changed socks for the first time in 4 days. Omer brought a small battery-operated radio from home. We tried to listen but there were some reception issues.

09:10 – Over the combat radio, the brigade's status report began. It was nice to listen and understand the full picture. They mentioned in the report that there was serious talk of a ceasefire soon for a prisoner exchange. I understand that's the direction it's heading in, but I really hope not. We need to continue fighting until Hamas no longer exists.

The situation with the hostages is horrifying. It's tough and complex. If we do not dismantle Hamas, this situation will likely recur. All terrorist organizations must know that when they deal with the State of Israel, they will be obliterated, and that's how we will prevent such events from happening in the future.

I cut an electric cable, exposed it, built an antenna from it for the radio, and we managed to hear various songs on Galgalatz.²³ What fun it was. It feels a bit disconnected from the fighting, for better or worse.

I went up to replace Yemini on guard duty. From the observation post, I suddenly saw a convoy of two tanks, two D9 bulldozers, and soldiers securing them as they moved towards the school. The D9s started to set up large batteries around a tunnel opening, seemingly preparing it for a detonation.

Nahman returns from an officers' meeting and tells us that we have a new mission: identifying and destroying weapons and tunnels in a compound belonging to a Hamas family, several of whom were Hamas naval commandos who took part in the Black Shabbat, October 7th. Lots of us wanted to go on this mission, but this time they told me to stay behind. I was really disappointed, but then Suedi declared with a smile, "It's ok guys, we'll have the time of our lives here." There's no one like Suedi. Sometimes he has his moments, but in general, he always creates a good atmosphere.

We are informed over the radio that there are ten minutes left until the detonation of the tunnel entrance. We need to leave the building and take everything "explosive," in case there is a tunnel under the building connected to the one they are blowing up. We take on all the explosives: four LAW missiles, grenades, mortars, and breaching charges.

---

23 A popular Israeli radio station, operated by IDF Radio.

On the way back, we passed another site that the Eshel team was at. There, they found an underground rocket launching system, under some orange and lemon trees, operated remotely by a mechanism located in a private house. I was stunned by the unimaginable fact that people are willing to risk the lives of their children and families by placing missiles and explosives in their backyards. I think about how careful we are, even among soldiers, to adhere to procedures related to explosives and demolitions, not to mention the caution around civilians and children. In our world, if a child is injured from exposure to explosive materials, it's a disaster, and their parents are considered criminals and negligent. This isn't the first time that we saw such things in Gaza, and unfortunately, it won't be the last.

In the afternoon, back at our stronghold, we eat and fix all the windows. Nahman briefs us, and it turns out that the ceasefire will take effect tomorrow morning. We are to be the last ones from the entire brigade to pack up and leave, something that I am a bit concerned about, as it is very likely that the enemy will be alert to our movement after so many soldiers have moved out. The goal is to be the last ones to move and to lay down heavy fire right before we pack up. Yemini and I suggested blowing up the stronghold we were in. It wouldn't require much: 2-3 explosive charges, 8 gas balloons, and sealing the building. Nahman proposed that we name the stronghold "Avi's House." Avi Buzaglo was a member of our team who went through training with us and later became a commander in one of the unit's companies. At the end of his military service, he joined the police force. He was a resident of Ofakim, a community on the Gaza border. On October 7th, when he realized what was happening, he went out to fight the terrorists with bravery and was killed during the tough battles in the city. We were very moved to commemorate him here.

The moment that we realized we were approaching a ceasefire, various thoughts went through our minds. So far, the army has not been able to do much about the hostages, and every passing day is critical. We are also eager to see the hostages released. However, we cannot escape the thought that Hamas is playing us, and more so – it is clear to us that after the ceasefire, the next time we face Hamas, they will be better prepared for us, and likely, there will be more casualties and injuries among our forces.

A discussion arose within the team questioning whether it's preferable to rescue a hostage at the cost of losing soldiers. After all, none of us are career fighters. We are well aware of why we are here, and we will do everything we can to save and release the hostages, but the situation nevertheless triggered these thoughts. We feared that the ceasefire would greatly harm the achievements of the war, not to mention that it would return power to the hands of Hamas. Generally, I have a feeling that Hamas will play us and only release foreign workers and no Israelis.

I spoke to some of the guys today about returning to our normal lives. I don't know how I'll do it. I feel very significant right now. Despite the chaos, everything is very clear to me: it is clear who is evil and who is good, clear why we are doing what we are doing. Every action has meaning. I'm living as an emissary, afraid of the moment of return to routine. A moment of anger over small things, of lack of appreciation for all the good I have in life.

Today, I'll be thrilled if they simply allow me to take off my vest. If I have rice for dinner – an indulgence. Just give me the chance to hug the woman I love. Even taking a shower is a rose-tinted dream. In short, I'm afraid of getting used to everything again. I want to continue getting excited about the little things. I want to continue living with a sense of purpose and action. If there's one thing important to me when we leave here, it's to get out of the rat race, to stop chasing after things that aren't really worth it. I want to focus on family, and with God's help, children. To be and do good. To be healthy and happy. To smile, to love.

It's almost 21:00, and I want to sleep a little. I wonder how our night will look. Currently, there's a lot of tank and artillery fire near our stronghold. I assume we will also be part of that later. Until then, good night!

Thursday, November 23, 2023

00:00 – I'm listening to the radio. Yemini wakes me up for guard duty, but I barely slept. There were loud attacks by our company until 21:15. Victor came to replace me because he needed to be on guard duty as well. I tried to fall asleep, but nothing helped. Many thoughts passed through my mind. About home, about Shiran, about the war, about the friends who were killed, about my soldier who was killed, about how surely, when everything ends, I'll find out about more friends who were hurt. I think about returning to routine and how to do it. Shlomi is guarding the position right next to me. There's no one like Shlomi. A soulful guy with a heart of gold, one of the funniest and quirkiest people. I spoke with him for a bit, and then Shaked came to him and said, "Listen, I can't sleep, let me switch with you." It was surprising because Shaked is a sleep freak. There wasn't a free moment that the guy didn't use for sleep. I could find him asleep on a pile of clothes and mess in the middle of the house while someone was stepping on him and it wouldn't bother him. He really showed impressive sleep capabilities that I envied every so often. Seems to me that his thoughts are also preoccupied.

Shaked and I started chatting. He asked why it's so important for me to write and remember everything. I told him that beyond the processing of experiences that writing gives, I feel that we are participating in something big and historical. I realize that I still can't grasp how big it is, but it's very important to me that, in a few years, when we can understand the magnitude of the event we took part in, I don't forget a single detail.

Suddenly, a loud explosion deafens our ears. A tank from our forces fired a shell very close to us without warning. Someone said something over the radio about seeing an enemy. But the truth is, the conversation with Shaked interested me more at that moment. We concluded on an important tip from Shaked: "Think of sleep as an inseparable part of the profession. A tired soldier is not professional." I agreed with every word of his. I tried again to fall asleep. In the background, the orchestra of the

IDF, composed of D9 engines, tanks, bursts of MAG and Negev machine guns, shoulder-fired missiles, and mortars. There was something calming about it. A uniform and deep rhythm of diesel engines alongside rumbles of machine guns creating a nice rhythm, accompanied by missile explosions.

Lately, the shooting has helped me fall asleep, like a pleasant melody in my ear. The noise distracts me from any thoughts until there is an explosion; I wake up again, go back to sleep, and it happens again. In the background, I hear someone saying that the ceasefire has been postponed, and we are staying here tomorrow.

10:55 – I wish I could explain how content I am right now. I'm sitting cross-legged, leaning on the dusty red couch in the site that has become our home for these past two days. The whole area is trembling from the noise of the tanks moving close to us. In the background, the radio is playing Ishay Ribo singing "Morning will rise, the sun will shine." Next to me is a cup of hot coffee, alongside a plate of warm hummus with fried onions and tahini on garlic bread. I am surrounded by my best friends. Could it get any better?

Amitai woke me up in the morning. The team is heading out for a mission that was planned yesterday, and I'm staying here with Suedi, Oz, and Dotan. I really wanted to go, but I'm also happy to stay here with these guys. In the morning, before the mission, we tidied up. We had a kind of patio, a roofless room that we turned into a garbage room, but it got a bit extreme so we decided to clean it. The problem was that it was truly disgusting. Bottles full of pee and more gross things. We looked at the huge pile of garbage we'd created in the last two days and didn't know where to start, so we just began. The moment you get your hands dirty, they're dirty, so it doesn't matter anymore – and then we were working on autopilot. Half an hour of work, and everything was clean. Suedi brought a bar of soap, we washed our hands with hand sanitizer, and returned to our routine.

We decided to take advantage of the time left before the mission to turn the bunker into "Avi's House," as Nahman suggested yesterday. Amitai sprayed "Avi's House" on the outer wall, with the symbol of our unit, Duvdevan, and a Star of David. The whole team stood by the wall with their equipment, Yemini unfurled the Israeli flag from his vest, we all stood strong, and Brown from the sniper team took a photo. Meir shared a few words about Avi. Tears welled up in my eyes, and my throat choked a bit.

The team leaves, and we stay behind. I went to cook hummus and make another coffee, and when Dotan finished putting on tefillin,[24] I took them from him and began to pray. In the background, on the radio, soldiers dedicate songs to their wives. I pray, "And you shall love the Lord your God slowly, slowly, with all your heart." Singer Arik Einstein's words enter my prayers. We clean up the location a bit more, sit for coffee, and talk. We sit and talk about life, conversations that help you understand how every single person is a world unto himself. Suddenly I think about the extent of the loss we've experienced as a nation, as families,

---

24 Phylacteries, a religious item worn by Jewish men during weekday morning prayers.

as friends. But at the moment, there isn't much space for that. There's a war to be fought.

We went down to chat with a small group of guys who stayed behind from the Kesten team. We talk a little politics, talk about why we got to where we are. Everyone agrees, from across the political spectrum, that we need to continue to fight until we eliminate Hamas and all the other organizations which took part in the terrible massacre on the seventh of October. Suddenly there is gunfire towards the stronghold. We all quickly grab our gear, trying to understand if it's our forces. Unable to verify, we pass our location number to the battalion so they don't confuse us by mistake and identify us as the enemy. Tanks passing nearby shoot towards the suspicious area. The firing stops after a few minutes.

Suedi takes the opportunity to throw a smoke grenade. We all understand that there isn't currently a need for the grenade, but Suedi took it today from Dotan and has been eager to throw it. He took out the pin and threw the smoke grenade into the palm tree near our location. Within half a minute, the tree catches fire. Suedi lost it. Suddenly, he began to stutter anxiously, literally frozen in place. "What am I going to do?" he said anxiously. "They'll definitely dismiss me, we need to go down now to put out the fire." Oz grabs a bucket and heads down. Suedi tells him, "Bring me Kuno, urgently. I need him."

From here to there, we found ourselves extinguishing a fire with a shovel and dirt. Within a few minutes, Suedi regained his composure, and we returned to the outpost, where we started to cook for the team. Biton tells us over the radio that a resupply should arrive soon, so I update the guys and return to sit with the Kesten team. Suddenly, the supplier comes on the radio, "I'll be at your position in a minute, if you're not there, we're gonna leave." Within seconds, I gather everyone who is in the stronghold and we head towards the intersection. We managed to arrive on time. We transferred the bags from the previous resupply and received the new supply bags. When we returned, we continued cooking food for the team. We cooked them a feast fit for kings – hot hummus, onion bread, garlic confit, fried onions, rice, pickled cucumbers, and sage tea. The guys arrived and were thrilled, and after everyone finished eating, we told them we also received letters from the families. Huge excitement. It's the kind of moment where everyone sits in silence and reads with tears in their eyes, or at least with a strong longing in their hearts.

I still haven't opened my letter, I was waiting for a slightly quieter moment. Besides, it's nice to know that you have something in your pocket that you know will make you happy. In the end, I found a quiet corner and read the letters from my parents and Shiran. It was truly moving and special. My friends made fun of me when they saw me with tears in my eyes. It became a team joke – every time someone gets emotional, they say that he loves his wife or something similar, and everyone laughs at him. But we all understand the meaning and strength that we receive from home.

We gathered for a night briefing. We sat around the radio in complete silence, listening expectantly for the announcer to talk about the prisoner exchange that's supposed to take place tomorrow. The moment he started talking nonsense, we turned it off. The battalion's operations officer explained to us what we should expect tomorrow. The plan is that at 04:00 we will begin our movement, at 07:00 arrive at the unit's base, and presumably then depart for a resort in Ashkelon. Like yesterday, today I also fear losing contact. Fear of the guys' surliness, or of some last minute mishap. In short, I hope that everything goes smoothly. I think that I'll go to sleep, I need to get up early tomorrow.

Friday, November 24, 2023

At 02:00 Amitai wakes us up. "Let's go, guys, get up. We're heading out to cover the whole division's exit." I quickly make some coffee for the guys. Truth be told, we didn't have much coffee left, but I wanted it to be enough for everyone, so it was a little coffee with a lot of water – what is professionally known here as "comrades' coffee." Clearly, it's not ideal, but at that moment, it was the most delicious coffee I've ever had.

Nahman is giving a briefing in the background, and shortly after that, we begin the maneuver. The goal that Yemini and I set for ourselves is to reach the cover area without sweating. We have all our gear on, and in addition, some guys took blankets with them. It's cold lying outside at night in the open for 3-4 hours without a blanket. I'm prepared for it to be very challenging. I put two heating packs in my pocket that I prepared in advance.

We leave the shelter and arrive at the grove area next to the school we had captured just two days ago. I brief the team and we begin the covering procedures. We stand facing the opposite direction of movement, protecting the forces heading out. Anyone with some understanding of warfare knows that one of the complex challenges is moving forces through forces, especially at night, as a fatigued soldier can easily mistake you for the enemy, and the risk of friendly fire is extremely high. This is especially true when it involves over two thousand soldiers in movement, so we mark our forces with stick lights and infrared lights. I activate the flashlight I have on my helmet with a flashing infrared light so they can identify us.

Relatively quickly, all the forces pass us by. It wasn't as cold as I feared. They tell us to dismantle the coverings, and then do the same for the unit's stronghold. By 07:00, we all need to reach the coastal road before the ceasefire begins.

We start the movement, with a convoy of APCs in the background. Suddenly, I see Victor sprinting towards Nahman. What's happening now? I ask myself. After a minute or two, the entire battalion stops in place. It turns out that Victor lost the transponder. It's a big mess. A very big mess.

The entire battalion stops in place. Very quickly, all the team's officers – Nahman, Oz, Victor, and I – return to where we were. The moment we arrive, Victor lights a red flare and finds the transponder instantly. You didn't have to be close to us to hear the sigh of relief that echoed at that moment. We quickly return to where the rest of the forces are and continue the movement. The sun begins to rise.

Thousands of soldiers move westward towards the sea. On our left is Beit Lahiya and Al-Atatra, in front of us is the sea, rows of tanks, and Israeli flags. We walk at a steady and fast pace. Shlomi and Meir say this is the hardest it has been since the beginning of the fighting. Walking at a very fast pace, with a heavy load. We reach the division headquarters. Massive batteries, huge quantities of fighters and officers. We all unload our backpacks and take a group photo.

There's a tangible feeling that the fighting has stopped. Pride, joy, laughter, relief, and a drop in tension. Suddenly, all the angst I had about the ceasefire disappeared. It's 06:58, and suddenly, in the background, we heard a shout: "3... 2... 1..." an enormous explosion shakes the whole neighborhood. A mushroom cloud of fire and smoke rises into the air at a height of several hundred meters. The smell of smoke rises in the air. Every guy with a camera is called to the flag. Team photos with the Israeli flag and war symbols in the background become the main activity. Gradually, a large cloud of smoke begins to cover the sky, and we all are covered in ash and dust, making the air hard to breathe.

We are informed that we are heading for a 24-hour break. It's a shame that the break is happening on Shabbat again, and once again the religious families will only be able to come for part of the time.

As soon as Rotem finishes the briefing, I ask him if I can spray a few things on the makeshift memorial that was along the coastal road. Rotem allows it. On October 7th, many of my friends fell in battle, including Avi Buzaglo and Ben Bronshtein. They were both amazing individuals, and even in these moments, I can't digest the fact that I'm talking about them in the past tense. I got to know Ben Bronshtein during my unit's training course, as well as in officer school, and we connected instantly. Ben was a special person. There was always a positive atmosphere around him; I never saw him without a smile on his face. Talented, cheerful, and handsome. Everywhere he went, he stood out. A good friend, a person who knew how to be sensitive to his surroundings. As I write about him, I start to cry and grieve. He was truly one of the best. Ben, like my good friend Avi, also fell on October 7th. He was among the first to fight and, unfortunately, among the first to fall.

I looked for a large place to spray their names. I wanted everyone passing by to see the names of these angels. I approached the memorial where I wrote in large letters, "In memory of the unit's fallen." I added the Duvdevan insignia and the names of Ben Bronshtein and Avi Buzaglo. Yemini and I looked at the wall one last time, gave a quick glance towards the sea, and returned to where all the team members were waiting to board the jeeps heading toward Israel.

On the drive out, I waved the Israeli flag until it flew off the makeshift pole it was attached to. We arrived at the Zikim base, where all the commanding officers were waiting for us, happy to meet each one of us. After a short while, we also received our cellphones.

I immediately called Shiran, my parents, and Shiran's parents. I missed them all so much. While we were all talking with the families, Dekel distributed more letters written by the families and the wives. These letters are something special. My mom tells me that my dad and Tzion will come to visit. Shiran says how much she misses and loves me, that she is getting things together and will come immediately, she just needs to figure out how to get here since she doesn't have a car. I try to sort it out. In the end, it was decided she would take a taxi to Jerusalem and then travel in a friend's car. Thank you so much, Odeya and Rafael; I truly appreciate it. It's not the first time friends have come to help, and it is just as moving each and every time.

The team boards the buses and travels to the resort. We unpack our gear and start getting ourselves together. I call Noa, an amazing woman from Ashkelon who also helped us during our last departure from Gaza. I ask her if there's a chance she could help us with laundry. Within minutes, Noa connected me with dozens of people who offered to take care of our laundry, cooking, pampering us, and really sorting everything we could dream of. I get a massage from one of the volunteers who came, and then Shiran arrives. What joy! We went to the marina, strolled around a bit, and then my dad and Tzion arrived, and we sat down to eat shakshuka and fresh pitas. Yitzhak, Shiran's dad, brought a lot of food that Galia, Shiran's mom, cooked, just the way I love it. We called Rabbi Stav to ask for his advice about Shiran staying with me in Ashkelon and returning to her base while it was still Shabbat.[25] When he said it was possible I was overjoyed! For seven weeks, Shiran and I hadn't been able to have a Shabbat meal together, and now we'll have that privilege.

---

25 Driving is an activity which is not permitted on the Sabbath for observant Jews.

That evening, after Shiran returned to her base, I was so exhausted that I fell asleep immediately. No blanket, with my clothes and shoes on.

Shabbat, November 25, 2023

When you're in a war for so long with the same group of guys, you slowly start to exhaust topics of conversation, and then the strange game of ranking the soldiers in the company begins. Of course, the Eshel team leads by far – they're a team of models. Each one is better looking than the next.

We are waiting to go back into battle, and meanwhile, they ask us to move because they need to land a small aircraft for reconnaissance photography during combat. Two soldiers from the "Sky Rider" unit arrive to fly the aircraft, and during the aircraft's takeoff, it relies on a stretched rubber cable. The soldier secures the cable, connects it to the aircraft, and steps back. All of us start cheering him on, but he is told that there is an issue. Five minutes later, the soldier tries his luck again. Once again, we all cheer him on. This time, the take-off is approved; he launches the aircraft, and we lift the soldier onto our shoulders, cheering enthusiastically. It seems to be the highlight of his service. Luckily, Dekel photographed the event.

The guys from the 551st Armored Brigade arrive and tell us that we have ten more minutes until we board armored personnel carriers to head into Gaza. I spoke with Or, our HR commander, about the earaches that have been bothering me since Beit Hanoun, and the back pain from last Friday's accident. She said to me, "There is no way that you're going into Gaza like this. You're going to the emergency room immediately for a check-up." And so, in a split second decision, I find myself in Arusi's Mazda, together with Dekel, on my way to the hospital.

A nurse sees me, and from there, I try to pass through all the stations as quickly as possible. Orthopedist, ENT, X-ray. Between the stations, I argue with the doctors to get them to note that I'm fit and able to return to the field. I come out and see that part of the recommendations in the discharge letter is for 15 days of rest. I return to the desk and ask them to remove the recommendation. They print a new summary for me, this time without the recommendations. I am discharged from the hospital, ready to return to battle, but my buddies are already in Gaza. Tomorrow morning, I have a hearing test at a military clinic down south, so I take the opportunity to spend the night at my parents'.

Sunday, November 26, 2023

3rd Outing

Shiran joins me, and we arrive at around 02:00 in the night. My sweet sister, Tzion, is still awake, waiting for us to arrive. We say goodnight to Mom and Dad, chat for a bit, and then head to bed.

In the morning, I hear my dad leaving for his teaching job

at school. I quickly get up from bed to say good morning, pray, and shower. Mom prepares delicious pancakes for us with butter and maple syrup. Miriam the cutie, my nine-year old little sister, waited for us and hadn't gone to school yet, so I accompanied her in my uniform.

We arrive at school together; I escort Miriam to her classroom, where she is excited, a bit shy, yet full of pride. All the kids are thrilled, the teacher sheds a tear. I see Miriam beginning to cry, so I call her outside for another hug. She hugs me as tight as she can and then adds, "Nani, please take care of yourself. It's hard for me with all of you at war. Promise me you'll come back." I promise. Suddenly, I understand the reality she's grown up in, with her three older brothers fighting on the most significant fronts of the war, and her two sisters-in-law currently serving in the military. This reality has forced her to mature. She's still the same sister I know, but with a much more complex understanding of the world. Suddenly, she's facing the possibility that not everything will be okay, not everything will be rosy, and she has to deal with it all the time. Her parents are tense at every phone call and knock on the door. She hears the news, all the rumors, and the worries of her friends; she sees families evacuating their homes in the area. She helps prepare the safe room at home. Like all of us, she understands that nothing will ever be the same.

I enter the classroom where my dad teaches. I say hello to all the students, telling them that they lucked out with the best educator. Amidst all the noise and excitement of the kids about my gun and uniform, I manage to notice a sparkle of pride in my dad's eyes. It's one of the feelings I love the most, knowing that I make my dad proud.

From there, I return home to pick up Shiran, say goodbye to my mom, Tzion, and Dror, and we head to the military clinic down south. During a hearing check, I'm advised to stay home for a steroid treatment, but I refuse. My team comes first. I've got to rush to join the convoy entering Gaza at 13:30, and it's already 11:00.

We first head to Beersheba, because it's crucial for me to buy a GoPro camera before I go into Gaza. I see value in documenting the combat. We enter a mall in Beersheba, and as soon as we step in, I hear a serious argument and curses coming from one of the shops. I enter the commotion and shout, "Aren't you ashamed? I've just come from Gaza, and in an hour, I'm going back, and the only reason I went to fight was so that things here would be okay!" Silence follows, and I add, "Come on, apologize to each other." Several older women who were watching start crying with excitement; one approaches me, crying, hugs me, and thanks me. I feel like I made a little difference in the world.

After buying the GoPro, we head to the Zikim Base. Shiran deals with setting up the GoPro on our way, and I'm a bit impatient because I want her to finish so that we can have a normal conversation. We get to the base, wait half an hour for supplies to arrive, and when they come, we say goodbye. Despite all the difficulties she faces, Shiran is still full of strength. I board the convoy heading to Gaza. While stuck in the traffic of tanks and armored vehicles, I take out the GoPro and enthusiastically start filming. We continue to progress slowly as we give out supplies to the various companies, until we get to the 9th Company. Wow, I'm excited to see the guys: despite only leaving them for less than 15 hours, I feel disconnected.

After Nahman's evening briefing, I go to Suedi and share my struggles with him. I expected him to tell me that everything was fine, but instead, he says, "Well, I didn't expect this from you. You've become soft." In an instant, my whole world turned black. Why did I try so hard to come back here quickly? Maybe I need to go back home altogether? I wanted to ignore Suedi, but I was so hurt and frustrated. What do they think, that I'm delicate? They don't know that I forced all the doctors to approve my quick return to the team. I confided in Suedi about what was bothering me, and he immediately apologized and clarified, "Honestly, I thought you'd be given mandatory bed rest, and you would still come back here as quickly as possible." I calm down. Getting ready for sleep, I'm tired and immediately sink into a good sleep. During one of the shifts, the Feuer Team comes on the radio and says they spotted a paraglider landing about 450 meters away from us. It undoubtedly raised our level of alertness and preparedness, but we didn't hear anything more about it later.

Monday, November 27, 2023

In the morning, we woke up to a rainy day, so we focused a lot on preparing the stronghold for the rain. We immediately used plastic sheets and wooden poles to cover the windows. Our new stronghold is inside a building that is still under construction, so besides the windows, it also has a lot of openings, which require a lot of work. After sealing the house, we went to set up a sniper position and improve the shelter. Outside our building, there is a large olive grove that poses a threat to us, so we asked the D9 to remove it. While the D9 started working, Yemini and I went to the Batzal Team's site to prepare improvised explosives to disperse amongst the axes that Hamas might use against us. We prepared 30 high-grade improvised explosive devices: pipe bombs, bottle bombs, improvised claymore mines. The devices were made up of explosive material and nails. I built a large claymore bomb composed of large pipe connectors. Inside, I packed 4.5 kilograms of explosive material, inserted 3 half-empty water bottles to surround the explosive material, as water greatly intensifies the explosion force, and added 3 kilograms of nails and bolts in an orderly manner. I sealed the charge from the other side, and made a small opening for the explosion at the back of the charge, and I cannot describe how proud I was of it. We joked about how in civilian life and in war you become proud of completely different things.

It took us two hours to lay all the charges. Although you always want to see how the charge you created works, I really hope we don't find ourselves in a situation where we have to use them, because that means that the enemy has come too close to our stronghold. But if it does happen, we will unleash them in a storm. We didn't manage to lay all the prepared charges by the time darkness fell. We preferred to leave the area before nightfall because we were warned of the possibility of a terrorist attack. In the event that they come, it's better for us to be inside the stronghold and use the defense positions that we built.

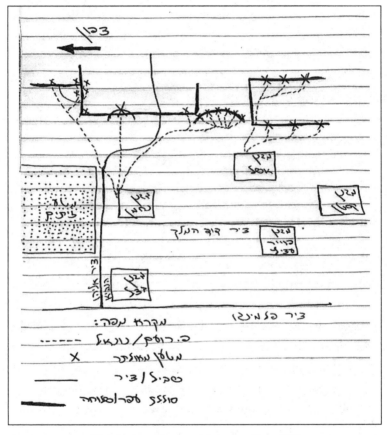

"Explosives Area – Al-Atatra Front"[26]

---

26 This drawing depicts the location of the teams (the rectangles), axes (the lines), olive grove (rectangle with dots), and the IEDs that we set up (the x's).

We thus returned to the strongholds. Outside, we managed to see the amazing work that the D9 had done. It hurts a bit to see the olive grove simply wiped out, but I now felt much more secure knowing that no one could sneak up on us from there. Nahman gave a night briefing, and then Yemini and I went to eat some leftover schnitzel and potatoes from the dinner meal supply.

We got ready for sleep, with our vests on. It was a cold night. During the hours when we were concerned about a potential terrorist attack, we added another defense position.

Tuesday, November 28, 2023

05:00 AM – Kaneti woke me up for guard duty. It was cold. I did some squats to warm up. After a minute of working out, the body warms up enough and stops shivering, so I do this every few minutes until the guard duty is over. When the guard duty ended, it was dawn-time. The sun hasn't fully risen yet, but as soon as there is light, the tiredness disappears. Of course, I'm always able to fall asleep, but it's no longer a challenge to stay awake. Since it's still the time of the "dawn protocol," the sniper post on the roof was manned. I went up to greet them and take all sorts of nice pictures. Dotan and Shlomi were at the post, and after a few minutes, Amitai joined. It was beautiful on the sniper's rooftop, especially because their observation post faces east, towards the rising sun. I stayed with them for a few minutes.

Amitai pointed out the location of his marriage proposal in the Gaza Envelope. I tried to take photos with my GoPro so that they would have an emotional memento, but I couldn't get good quality pictures. After taking a few pictures of them, I went downstairs and drank my morning coffee. Of course I burnt my tongue. I murmured to myself: this too shall pass.

Suddenly, I recalled a funny moment from the night. At around 03:00 in the morning, Meir woke me and Yemini up for guard duty, and when we arrived at the post, Shaked also arrived. Meir was surprised, asked him what he was doing here, and Shaked answered, "You woke me up for guard duty." After a half-minute, Michaeli join us, and the same thing happened again. Half a minute later, Suedi joined the party. It turns out that Meir, feeling drowsy, "invited" two extra guys due to his exhaustion. It was a funny moment because Meir suddenly realized what he had done and got really flustered. Very quickly, Shaked the sleep champion and Michaeli went back to sleep.

At 07:30, Lahad entered and called for Nahman and Victor. It turns out that the Feuer and Batzal teams are going out for R&R (rest and recuperation). We are number three in the priority list for leaving the Strip, because we have many married men and fathers on our team, but there is currently no approval for three teams to leave the company. Lahad came to ask Nahman whether it was possible for six soldiers to leave and the rest to stay. Nahman thought it would be better for everyone to stay, but after consulting with Victor, they decided to allow the six to leave. I think it was the right decision. It was clear to everyone that Meir, Oz, and

Amitai were leaving because they have children. The guys are looking at me.

Yes, I'm married, but just two days ago, I left for a doctor's appointment. Although it only gave me an extra 15 hours at home, I clearly felt that some of my comrades deserved the break more. It was a very tough moment, because I couldn't help but think about how Shiran would feel if she knew that I had the option to leave, but I gave it to another team member? Shiran has told me several times, "You always say that the team is important, but what about me?" And her words have been etched in my heart. I am truly willing to do anything for her. But I also feel obligated to my nation and to the values that I was brought up on: to love and serve the Jewish people and its land. That's what we are fighting for. It was a flood of emotions that concentrated into silent contemplation, of a prayer that I am making the right decision.

Nahman looks at me with full understanding, and I feel that he is feeling the same, because he too is a commander. I really wanted him to leave, but Nahman dismisses me with a wave of the hand. I know that even though his hand movement was light, it was heavy in his heart. I felt it through his eyes. We told Kashi and Kaneti to go home, and we saw on their faces how much they needed it. Both of us take a deep breath, and the discussion continues. Who's going out?

Suedi just then wakes up and with his typical smile says, "Don't mess around. If no one else is going out, I'll take it." The guys who are leaving are getting their things together, and we share in the collective happiness. I go up for guard duty and switch with Meir so that he can organize his things. Everyone comes to give hugs before they leave, and I'm happy for them, and I pray that Shiran doesn't feel hurt. When I come down from guard duty, we all sit down to have breakfast. In the background, the Galgalatz radio blasts on the highest volume to distract our thoughts. But today, Galgalatz has decided that all the songs will be about home… I laugh and think to myself, who is actually listening to them? IDF soldiers and families of hostages. We had plenty of time to relax. The house is quiet without all the teams, but we quickly return to our routine.

Earlier today, Victor found a hookah. Suedi, Victor, and I went to search for flavoring, coals and tinfoil. We found the flavoring relatively quickly, but couldn't find coals for the hookah, so we took coals from the barbecue, and after a few minutes of searching, we found tinfoil. From there, we moved towards the Kesten team stronghold, and we sat with them for a few minutes. The truth is, their site seemed admiratively structured. Furnished, with a kitchen, even flooring. They took great care to clean it thoroughly. There was a good atmosphere. Some of us smoked hookah, some played the card game Yaniv, some relaxed in the rooms, and some kept watch. I really like the Kesten team. They're always nice, always create a good atmosphere. On the way back, Suedi did graffiti on one of the ruined houses and wrote, "Is Kono here? Has anyone seen Kono?" It's a bit of a private joke within the team. Yemini calls me "Kono" instead of "Kuno," and everyone laughs about it and imitates him. Since they started imitating him, that sentence gets thrown into the conversation every few minutes.

I'm called "Kuno" after my great grandfather. He

was called Elkana Roth, but everyone always called him "Kuno." Unfortunately, I didn't know him, but before I enlisted in the army, I told Saba Chaim, his son, that I'd introduce myself as Kuno when people asked me my name, and when I go to officer course and return to the unit, I'll be the leader of "Team Kuno." And indeed, that's how it was. For the final ceremony of my combat training, I made sure to bring Saba Chaim. He was moved by the fact that a team was named after his father, and I was also moved – by the privilege of making my grandfather proud. When we finished the ceremony, I stepped down from the stage and presented him with a Team Kuno shirt. When I was discharged, Grandpa once jokingly asked, "Is that it? No more Team Kuno?" So I assured him that I would think of something. Shortly after being released from service, I started a youth training business, named "Kuno." Here, in the middle of Gaza, I'm prouder than ever that my grandfather's name continues to accompany me.

After taking a few photos next to a truck that was struck by a shell, we return to the stronghold. In the shelter, we meet some of the guys including Elad "Ollar," the battalion operations commander. In one of the resupplies, he spoke to me about his love of climbing. Aside from Elad, there were also Vax, the deputy battalion commander's radio operator, and Benyamini, the deputy battalion commander, who was the company commander before Rotem. Today he owns a start-up in Miami, but when he heard the news on October 7th, he packed up everything and came.

We tried to understand from the guests if there was talk of an imminent departure, but we didn't hear anything concrete from them. We all sat together at the center of the table with a hookah. A few songs, and each of us speaks a bit about life outside. After the conversations, the guys from the remote command center left, and I went up for guard duty. During guard duty, I played with the "Tomer," a thermal device I didn't know about before the war. It has many advantages over the "Armon," which we had until now. It has superior enemy identification capabilities and heats up much faster. During guard duty, I identify, through the "Tomer", a guy looking in our direction from behind a curtain, in a building very far from us. There is no chance that he can see us. I take pictures and record the building as a potential target for when the ceasefire ends. When I finished the surveillance, I went to eat the chicken and gnocchi that came with today's resupply. It was tasty but cold.

After eating, we talked again. Each person shared a hobby that we didn't know about. I said that I love baking and cooking. I told them about my tradition of sitting with Dolev, Aviv, and Shiran on Shabbat mornings for coffee and cake before prayers. It's been eight Shabbats since we last did that, since my quick coffee with Dolev on that Black Shabbat. Michaeli told us that he loves hosting, but that during the war, he discovered he hasn't got a lot of experience with DIY tools. Shaked shared that he loves ceramics and clay. Suedi said that he recently started to love yoga, and Shaked added, "I actually just started meditation." Omer said he loves taking ice baths. I love Omer, a quiet guy with a big heart. In the past, when guys used to bug him, he'd explode, but now, I feel like I'm with a different person. It seems like he recently underwent a deep change. Omer attributes it to ice baths. And so everyone shared something. It was pleasant being all together, but as time went by, the feelings of happiness for the guys who had gone home quickly turned into envy.

Wednesday, November 29, 2023

A choir of dogs barked all night. The wind howled. This time there were no explosions and no sounds of war – just a ceasefire. There's something slightly scarier in this silence. We know Hamas is setting up observation posts, sniper positions, and anti-tank teams. If they want to, they can open fire on us in an instant. When our partners in the ceasefire agreement are murderers, rapists, kidnappers, antisemites, ruthless and wild people, you know it's only a matter of time before they decide to break the agreement and exploit the situation to their advantage. That's how our guard shifts pass. It was very cold at night, and to warm up, I drank tea and hot water. For some reason, I couldn't fall asleep.

In the morning, I woke up to do guard duty from 04:00 to 05:00, and then we started our "dawn preparations," so I stayed awake. We organized the stronghold, ate, and Nahman gave a briefing. Suddenly, the fact that we are here while half the team was at home became really tough, and it was especially hard when I thought about my Shiran.

Later, in the late morning hours, Biton came onto the radio and informed us that we have packages waiting for us at the brigade commander's house. Nahman asked who was going, so Omer and I volunteered. We expected to arrive and see many large packages, but when we got there, we saw four small boxes. I was a bit disappointed. Did we really expose ourselves for 600 meters to get these tiny packages? We split the boxes among ourselves according to the team names written on them, and from there we returned to our stronghold. It smelled horrible on the way. It seemed like some D9 buried a cow carcass there. The scent of death.

When we returned to the shelter, we opened the package and discovered a box of fried eggplants, a box of hard-boiled eggs, a box of potatoes, tahini, a bunch of parsley, and pitas. In short, an amazing Sabich package. It came just in time. Sabich is a comforting food.

We noticed that we were all completely worn out. Nahman announced that everyone would go on a patrol in the sun to change the atmosphere. It was important. We headed towards the observation company and went up to their site. It was crazy to observe Beit Lahiya. You could actually see inside the houses for up to four kilometers.

When we returned to the shelter, I was completely exhausted. I dozed off for about two hours. It was incredible. I think that a lot of the frustrated feelings I had were due to exhaustion. Waking up, I remembered I hadn't put on tefillin today, so I washed my face and hands. All the guys sat down to eat a hot lunch from the resupply. I looked at the room, and it had changed completely. While I was sleeping, they had cleaned and arranged the stronghold, and spread tarps and rugs on the floor. The shelter looked significantly better.

Victor told me that in ten minutes I was replacing him on guard duty. Sunset was happening at any minute, so I quickly put on tefillin. While on duty, Rotem decided that our patrol was too quiet, and even though we're in the middle of a ceasefire, we need to instill some deterrence. I agreed with him.

Omer and Shaked from the Negevists, and Yemini the MAGist, ran outside our stronghold, shooting towards the bullet trap, just to give a sense of an "attack." From what I understand, beyond coordinating this with the battalion and the brigade, we also coordinated with a visual intelligence unit to attempt to identify enemy movements during the shooting. Tank smoke also obscured the whole area to the east of us.

Suddenly I saw the tank driving north towards us, passing between us and the area where we planted bombs. I got nervous. It was obvious that during his drive, he tore apart all the explosives that were supposed to activate and set off the charges that we'd prepared. But I had no way to check that at that moment, and by the time I finished my guard duty, it was already dark. We can only hope that Hamas won't try to do anything before tomorrow morning, and I'll check the state of the charges then.

The time right now is 22:50; in ten minutes, I finish my first guard shift of the night. It's much less cold tonight, so I fell asleep relatively quickly. When Yemini called me for my next shift, I was exhausted and asked for another minute to get up. When I got up, I put a tea kettle on the stove.

We do hour-long guard shifts, with each being split into two parts: the first half-hour in the northern position and the second half-hour on the radio. I scanned the area with the "Tomer" and identified a camel about 580 meters away from us. Besides that, more of the same. In the background, Radio Jerusalem talks about the hostages and the ceasefire. I ache for all those families. It's comforting to be in Gaza at this time; it distances you from the mourning and the pain. It might sound weird, but that's how I feel. I remembered that Nahman said that the battalion's reconnaissance team is supposed to replace us tomorrow. I'm really looking forward to that, but I don't fully believe in my heart that it will happen. I finished my guard duty; I'm going back to sleep.

Thursday, November 30, 2023

02:17 – This is my second guard shift of the night. Some might say this hour is random, but all those who understand the real meaning of the number in question are part of a respectable and special club (and if you still don't get it and are curious and determined, turn to p217).

I'm always debating what to do with all that I've written. I'll definitely keep it; after all, it's an amazing way to remember the war, but I've considered maybe publishing a book. Who would have believed that Elkana Cohen, the most academically-challenged student around, would write of his own volition? Here, people sometimes call me A.D. Gordon.[27]

---

27 A renowned Zionist thinker and leader.

In elementary and high school, I used to turn in blank tests because I didn't have the energy to write. It was painful for me, and when I did write, it was full of spelling mistakes. To this day, mistakes have been a constant companion of mine, but they don't stop me from writing. There were times during exams when I'd raise my hand to ask how to write a specific letter. I would try to write the letter aleph and just couldn't. I had every "dys": "dysgraphia," "dyslexia," and so on... However, it now seems like all of the arguments with my parents paid off. Their arguments with me, and the long hours "spent" at parent-teacher meetings and talks, did their job.

I was an irritable child. Throughout my childhood, even in moments when I yelled at my parents (I'm embarrassed to write that I sometimes really screamed at them), they had one response that they repeated like a mantra. I would say to them, "Leave me alone," and they would hug me tightly and say, "Elkana, we will never give up on you." I was a relatively strong child and I tried to escape from home, but my parents would hug me and not let me move. In the morning, when I saw my mom, she would tell me, "Elkana, you almost broke my fingers yesterday, but it's important to me that you know that we will never give up on you."

I remember one day, when I was already in the army, my mother came to talk to me after I had an anger episode. She said "Elkana, it's too difficult now for me and Dad to hold on to you. We're here for you always, but you're too strong. If you don't learn to control yourself, you'll grow up to be an angry person. It's bearable as a child, but as an adult, being irritable – there's nothing good about it. It's just not nice to be around. Believe me, Elkana, you don't want to be that kind of person."

That conversation gave me a serious shock. It wasn't that I suddenly became a calm person, but I became much more self-aware. I understood that anger and frustration often stem from a feeling of lack of control in a situation. For example, if you're driving on a road and suddenly your tire blows out, it can really annoy you, but... if you knew at the beginning of the drive that your tire would blow out in 10 minutes, when it happens, it wouldn't surprise you, and I'm sure you'd be less irritated. That's how I started to operate. I would ask myself what could surprise me or what could go wrong now, and when it happened, I wouldn't get angry. I think the most significant change I made was since I met Shiran. I have a lot more progress to make, but today I think that I'm in a much better place.

At 05:00, Nahman wakes us up. After a minute of denial, I get out of the sleeping bag to the morning's tranquility. I warm up by a pot filled with coals and listen to the battalion radio. The battalion commander reports that the ceasefire will end at 07:00 and there's talk that Hamas will likely strike earlier to catch us off guard. The commander updates us that there's a planned brigade-wide strike on all the targets that we found last week.

At 06:00, I start guard duty, and there's high operational tension. Yemini and I both agree that now is the ideal time for Hamas to strike. The sun blinds us, and we can barely see to the east. I have a certain apprehension, although I know that no matter what happens, they truly stand no chance against us. I bring the shock tube detonator (Nonel) closer so I can initiate the setups we prepared (hopefully the tanks didn't destroy them yesterday) in case Hamas forces decide to test us. My shift continues, and suddenly on the radio, the broadcaster says, "The ceasefire will continue..." Wait, what? We were sure we'd be engaging in combat within 5 minutes. The battalion commander updates us that the ceasefire will continue until tomorrow, but since it's possible that some of the Hamas fighters may not receive the update, they might try to attack. Additionally, he informs us that we will most likely be leaving for home at 14:00, so we're trying to expedite procedures ahead of the exit. The reconnaissance team is supposed to replace us with a fresh force, and we don't want to leave them with a site full of explosives. So, Yemini and Nahman go to disassemble the five setups. At least we tried building charges and setting up the sites.

At around 15:00, the Rico team arrived to replace us. We began moving towards the unit's headquarters, where the transport unit was waiting for us.

The itching to get home was palpable. We wanted to get out of there quickly, but as always, there were delays. Every minute felt like an eternity. Sitting in the Humvees, half of us already had no feeling in our legs due to the heavy load and weight of the bags placed on us, and of course, right when we found a comfortable position, Yemini made us all get up so that he could urinate.

Finally, we left. We arrived at Camp Bilu, and within seconds, we were all ready – all the equipment inside the vehicles after we passed a short inspection chain including optics, weaponry, and logistics. Nahman and Kesten gave a departure brief, and asked us to be mindful not to drive while being tired, to update them that we had arrived home safely, and to rest. 'Ah,' they added at the end. 'We've just been asked now to tell you, that there's a chance we're returning on Shabbat morning.' We were incredulous. We said that it probably wouldn't happen and hit the road. At 20:15, I arrived at home. First things first, a shower.

Friday, December 1, 2023

It's the early afternoon. Shiran and I are just returning from a luxurious breakfast we had in the Ra'anana Park by the lake. So far it has been amazing. We managed to eat, talk, and most importantly, listen and pay attention to what each of us has been through in the recent period. We were just leaving the car towards our home to prepare for the Shabbat morning meal, and suddenly Shiran starts to cry and tells me, "Elkana, it's happening." She was holding my phone: we had just received a message to say that we're returning to the Bilu base tomorrow at 11:00, and on Saturday evening we're to enter Gaza.

It is very painful for me to see how hard it is for Shiran. I feel her pain. It is clear to all of us why we are doing what we are doing, but the longer the war lasts the less we feel that. Our lack of communication along with all the sad news updates make things difficult, and on top of all that, Shiran has also been serving in the reserves since the Black

Shabbat. She experiences a lot of challenging events and feels like she doesn't have anyone who truly understands her. I, supposedly by her side, am not available for her. Shiran serves in Duvdevan. Every wounding, killing, security and friendly fire incident passes through her. She feels that knowing everything that is happening in my unit will give her certainty, but we both understand that this is not reassuring for her. "There's nothing to be done," she tells me, "this is my way to cope."

Shabbat, December 2, 2023

4th Outing

Before I left home on Shabbat morning, we had a conversation that almost caused me to stay at home. It was very hard for me that Shiran was not doing well. But I told her that we are in the middle of a special period, and we need to remember the great privilege we have as Jews to defend ourselves. The beauty of Shiran is that no matter how hard it is for her, once the decision was made, the first thing she said was, "Elkana, it is important to me that you know that I am strong. I am sending you strength, and I am very proud of you for your decision." That's my Shiran. The woman who, in a moment, overcomes her personal difficulties and cultivates strength. I've seen this in her many times, and in the recent period, it is very prominent. I hugged her and we parted in peace.

At 10:05, Michael, a friend from the platoon who also

lives in Ra'anana, came to pick me up with his wife. We arrived at the base at 10:50, where the supply soldiers were waiting for us along with all our gear. We organized our personal gear, this time for 48 hours without a resupply. Everyone filled their packs with food, water, ammunition, winter gear, hygiene products, energy bars, field dressing kits, etc... By 13:15 we were already on the buses. We managed to switch to new tactical helmets that Aviv Atzitz's mother successfully arranged for the company.

When we got to Beit Lahiya, I took a black softshell jacket with me, but quickly realized that it was a poor choice, as a tired fighter could easily get confused and think I am the enemy because I'm wearing clothes that are not green. I knew that I had to get a military softshell, but the problem was that I didn't know where to get it. Our supply officers said there were none, and so did all of my friends. When I arrived at the base, I met a nice girl named Alin. After a few minutes of talking, I mentioned the issue of the softshell, and suddenly she tells me, "What a coincidence, I forgot that I have one in the office." She took care of it and gave me a high quality softshell.

Before entering, the brigade commander, Col. Ido Kas, arrived and spoke with us for 30-40 minutes. He talked about the achievements of the Brigade, the importance of what we are doing, that we seemingly have a maximum of another month, and that the current battle will hopefully end by Thursday. He talked a little about how he sees great importance in allowing soldiers to return home frequently.

At the end of the conversation with the brigade commander,

Nahman arrived to deliver an order to the team. The mission: to reach Jabaliya in the advanced battle and control the Adel axis for missions regarding the Indonesian hospital. We understand that we are to serve with the auxiliary company in the upcoming attack. Shabbat finishes and I manage to talk to Shiran, and I can already hear how much stronger she sounds. Right after I hung up the phone, I remembered that the first night of Hanukkah falls on Thursday, and it is very likely that I won't make it in time to light candles with Shiran. So, I asked one of the supply officers to send a message to my mother, asking her to send Shiran a bouquet of flowers on the first night.

We stood in a Het formation (picture a rectangle without one of the short sides) with the company commander, had a motivational conversation with the rabbi, and then a conversation with Lahad, and of course, how could we end without singing all together "Am Yisrael Hai". We also had a conversation with Jake, the company commander, and got guidance ahead of the trip with the armored personnel carrier (APC).

I went to look for grape juice for Havdallah, and since I didn't find any, I made Havdallah over Coca Cola. Waiting for them to update us on when to board the truck, time passes. And more time. Enough time for us to wander to some corner. Meir and Oz suggest going to the sports hall, and very quickly the entire team finds themselves in the hall–some playing basketball, some sleeping, and some just talking.

I understand that we are going to wait here for a long time, especially when I look around and see that the entire battalion is lying next to us, asleep. The moment I understood the situation, I opened my sleeping bag and went to sleep.

Sunday, December 3, 2023

At around 03:30 AM, we finally boarded the trucks, but not before passing through an HR checkpoint so we could cross the border. We took a team picture and hit the road.

At Camp Erez, we waited another ten minutes in the vehicles. Suddenly, we saw the destruction wreaked across the camp from that Black Shabbat: posts that had received direct missile hits, overturned roadblocks. The smell of a fire burning nearby sent shivers down my spine for a moment, giving life to the horrors that occurred there on that day. We headed towards the Gaza Strip, and the sounds of war returned. It had been several days since we'd heard it with such intensity. Air Force gunshots and bombings, artillery fire, and tank shots amidst ground operations of the D9. Next to Camp Erez we can still see defense positions that have been destroyed.

During the ride, I heard the guys say that this is the scariest entry we've had so far – and not because of the mission we're about to undertake. True, it's in the heart of enemy territory, and in addition, the ceasefire gave the enemy time to prepare for us; but we all know there's no mission we can't handle. The fear stemmed from the connection between the sights we had just seen at Erez and the atrocities that occurred on

October 7th. A massacre took place, and we weren't there to defend.

The power of these trucks is incredible, there's nothing they're not capable of. We sped along, with lots of bumps and jolts on the road. There are no seatbelts, so getting an elbow to the ribs becomes routine. Oz climbed onto the truck without a softshell jacket, and is now complaining about the cold. I curl up in mine.

We reached the gathering point. Hundreds of soldiers and dozens of tanks were already waiting on the ground. We quickly disembarked the vehicles and attached ourselves to one of the batteries near the auxiliary forces. We realized we needed to unpack our sleeping mats fast. I slept like a baby. Nahman nudged me and said, "Kuno, if you want to remove gear from the MAG, you're allowed to, because the axis is going to be a kilometer and a half instead of 150 meters." We had a feeling this would happen. We'd thought about leaving them behind, but in the end, we loaded our bags with the ammo boxes.

An hour and a half later, we were woken up. We performed our roll call and began moving. I said a prayer for a safe passage, put on my night-vision goggles and headed out. My heart raced, along with my senses. I took a few deep breaths and entered "combat mode." Weapon in both hands, scanning with my night-vision goggles in all directions, while striving to maintain proper distances during movement. Through my gun scope, I identify all the buildings. In the background, the sounds of war are escalating. The odors of corpses, fire, and gunpowder mix with the scent of citrus fruits. We are approaching our targets. The sun rises.

I understand where the citrus scent comes from. The axis we are walking along was part of an orange and clementine orchard, until last night, when tanks and D9s cleared the way for us. The moment I see the clementines, I approach the trees, pick and eat them. I offered some slices to Shlomi, but he refused – his loss. I tucked away an orange in my pocket. We were too close to our targets for me to start peeling an orange there and then.

We arrive at the built-up area, experiencing a slight delay in our maneuver. We enter a destroyed site and sit down there. I seize the opportunity to eat the orange. I don't know if it was because of hunger or thirst, but it was the tastiest orange I'd eaten in years. I gave half to Yemini and two more slices to Kaneti. I licked my fingers so they don't remain sticky for long. The taste of orange and the soot from my hands mix in my mouth. This might be the last time I do this. Maintaining hygiene here is a challenge, and this was a foolish move.

I take some photos for the team, and I'm stunned by the tremendous destruction in the neighborhood. We see a high-rise building split in half, with a sofa on the top floor overlooking the view. It would be nice to sit right now. We reach our strip. Nahman gives out orders. In the background, massive vehicles are sweeping for IEDs and creating a clear path for us to our site. Jake and Nahman give final briefings before entering combat, and we head out for the attack.

The Spear Squad leads and scans the ground floor as well as the underground level. Squad B, led by Suedi, captures the first floor, and our team does a more thorough scan for explosives. It turns out that while we took over the house, a soldier from our company was injured by shrapnel from a mortar that fell near our forces. Later on, we find the launch site that the enemy seemingly used for this attack.

The house was very clean and organized. Nearly all the homes we entered have been significantly impacted by gunfire and bombings. This house wasn't sparkling, but it was relatively well-maintained. As we searched, we found fresh food and a pot of coffee. It seems like the people living here had left just a few hours earlier. Our mission was to secure the targets from the south while the rest of the battalion engaged in combat. It took a long time for the battalion to advance, so we took advantage of this time to set up positions, rest, and pray. Somehow, of all the houses, this particular one didn't have gas. Victor lit boards inside a pot and prepared coffee. It nearly suffocated us. Within three minutes, the whole house was filled with smoke. We told him to throw the pot outside, and slowly the smoke subsided.

We have three strategic positions overlooking and controlling the entire southern strip perfectly. This explains why about 20 minutes after we finished capturing and clearing the building, we found ourselves surrounded by all levels of command in the brigade, from the brigade commander, to the battalion commander, to the company commander. We began a battalion-wide attack. From a distance, we identify various figures running between sites, and a Zik – an unmanned aerial drone with reconnaissance and attack capabilities – also identifies several terrorists mingling among civilians in the Adel axis area located to the south of us. We understand that this area is much more alert and active compared to the areas we have been in until now, and we are primarily preparing for encounters with terrorists. In one room, there are the brigade and battalion commanders, Shlomi and Amitai are at the sniper post. In the central room, Kashi and Meir are on the MAG, Michaeli is on the grenade launcher, and I direct them towards the targets, maintaining visual contact with the attacking forces. In the left room, Shaked and Omer are on the Negevs. Once we receive clearance to fire, Meir shoots the first bullet, followed by everyone else. This was our first firing of this outing.

After a long walk with heavy loads, it is clear to all of us that one of the objectives of the firing is to shoot a lot. The ammunition for the machine guns is very heavy, and Meir was determined to lighten the load. Within fifteen minutes, around 3.5 boxes of ammo were shot by the MAG, and between 2 to 3 boxes by the Negev, along with approximately 30 grenades and another 8-10 magazines of 5.56 ammo. According to my quick calculations, about 50 kilograms of ammunition were fired. Meir achieved his goal. During the shooting, we assess the targets and ensure that no terrorist dares to present himself while the assaulting forces, the 9th and 10th Companies, advance towards them. In addition to our gunfire, the Air Force, mortars, and artillery batteries bombarded the area throughout the night. The 9th Company engaged in combat and we ceased firing, except for precise shots from observers who confirmed the terrorists' presence.

The mission: to take control of the block controlling

the Adel axis. While the forces carry out the mission, we identify an observer running down the Lima axis and enter the "Block" – the Sheikh Zayed neighborhood. It's a matter of seconds, especially when a tank south of us activated a smoke screen that obscured our field of vision. Fortunately, Amitai was quick enough to shoot a single shot from the sniper. During the firefight, we spotted fire trucks and ambulances moving on the Adel axis. It is clear to us that these serve terrorists, but unfortunately, they're beating us in the battle for international legitimacy, and as long as there is no clearly visible threat, there is no authorization to fire. Near the Adel axis, south of the school where we identified many individuals, we realize there are many terrorists preparing for us. This situation makes me mad. This is a combat zone, and no civilian should be here.

They might present themselves as uninvolved, but let me tell you something. I've passed through their neighborhoods and their homes. Each of them has flags of terrorist organizations at home. Upon entering many houses, they proudly display images of "martyrs" who participated in the attacks and murders of Jews. Their neighborhoods are full of terror infrastructure. Enough, I'm fed up with all the gentle expressions. Those who choose to remain in the battlefield know what they are doing. I don't desire war, quite the opposite. I would very much like to have peace, but currently, I don't see any possibility for peace with a group of people who have kidnapped, murdered, and taken children, men, and women as hostages. The sun begins to set, and we need to advance towards the new battalion defensive position in the Sheikh Zayed, the neighborhood we just took over.

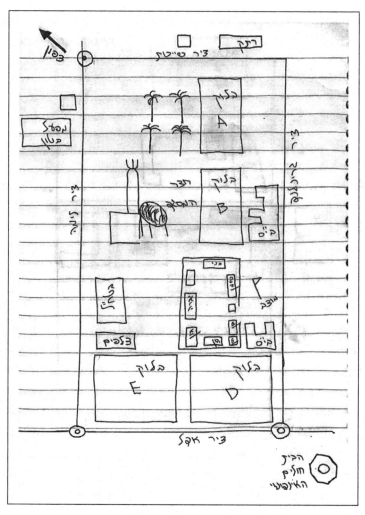

Sheikh Zayed Neighborhood, Jabaliya[28]

---

28 This drawing depicts the neighborhood of Sheikh Zayed, Jabaliya:
various buildings, axes with names, and the mosque from which a
terrorist emerged from a tunnel shaft. Hundreds of explosives were
found in these buildings.

We move through Block C. Around us are the other companies. In the building, we found all kinds of improvised pipe bombs and a 2 x 2 pallet used for launching mortars. Printed on the pallet were circles with degrees, and in the center an 'X' indicating the location for launching the mortar.

Some of the apartments looked as if the terrorists had just left them. As soon as we finished scanning, we started setting up a stronghold. Quickly, the entire team went into action. Every time I am amazed by how we can turn a disgusting area into a gem of the Sharon.[29] First, we seal the windows, then start throwing out all the unnecessary items. Kashi, as always, on the sweeping, Victor on the kitchen, Kaneti with the hammer and nails, and Michaeli wherever he's needed.

After an hour of work, we have 2 bedrooms, a living room, a glorious kitchen, a room used as a defense station, and a garbage room. Generally, I am against garbage rooms since we always end up with a stinky room in the end. It is better to throw everything out of the building from the beginning, but sometimes there is not enough time, so we wait for the morning hours to continue arranging the stronghold. Oz and Yimini installed lighting. After we finished organizing the place, Victor prepared a nice meal for us.

We'd had an intensive day and we were exhausted. Yemini felt sick all day, so we let him rest whenever possible. Suedi also didn't feel good. It turns out that

---

29 The name of the region of central Israel, which is considered beautiful and affluent.

during the night, Meir vomited his guts out. I also felt a bit dehydrated.

Monday, December 4, 2023

When we woke up in the morning, I made sure to drink water and began to feel like myself again. It turns out there was a resupply of just water during the night. I took advantage of the morning for writing and prayer, then went to bring more water with Victor and Shlomi. On the way back, I passed by the battalion's remote command center to contact Shiran on the Red Phone. I understood that she was okay from the sound of her voice. The commander told me there was no problem with talking to her, just to make sure to avoid military talk, mentioning locations, etc. When Shiran answered, immediately after she asked how I was doing, she said, "Elkana, I see you've set up a battalion stronghold near the Adel Axis. Are you watching out for yourselves?" I chuckled to myself. Of course, Shiran knows all of the details, nothing escapes her. We finished the conversation and I stayed to talk a bit with the command center until Victor called me and said we were going to scan two more buildings in Block C. Because I hadn't eaten yet, I grabbed a few protein bars and bread and hit the road.

It's just not normal how within a few minutes I was drenched in sweat. It's not that it's hot, but scanning all of these apartments is tough work. In the first apartment we entered, everything was burnt. When we tried to enter the northern room, to our surprise, we found that the entire room had collapsed. A quick look upwards revealed that all the rooms in the northern part of the building had collapsed. This is how we scan room by room. Most of the apartments are burnt, and what isn't destroyed is full of dust and debris. We find all kinds of Hamas and Fatah scarves, and move on to the second building, which is also half burnt.

During the scans, we find a locked apartment with the word "Danger" written on it in Arabic. We pass by it and make a note to blow it up later on, once we leave the stronghold. On the upper floor of the building, we find a hideout apartment that the enemies had occupied not long ago. It seems that they were prepared for combat. We found rifle bullets and quantities of food that could feed an entire team for several days. We decided to burn down the apartment, and within two minutes, massive flames burst out of the windows. Elad, the staff officer, shouted from the neighboring building, "Have you lost your minds? You're endangering all of our forces!" I thought he was exaggerating, but I let it go.

When we returned to our fortification, the first thing I did was take off my vest and helmet. I was dripping with sweat. The helmet was disgustingly soaked, so I placed it on the couch. When Shlomi arrived to sit on the couch, he moved the helmet and was shocked by the amount of sweat. Nahman arrived a few minutes later, visibly agitated, and said, "Because of Kuno and Oz, we need to vacate this stronghold." That pissed me off. There was no reason for him to make a statement like that. Both Nahman and Jake, the company commander of the auxiliary, approved the fire, so he shouldn't cast blame like that.

Within a few minutes, everyone became agitated, and the atmosphere became unpleasant. Later on, Jake arrived and took responsibility, and said that his team should have thought a bit more before acting. Personally, I don't think it was such a problem, and it seems that Elad getting upset at some of the team members created a chain reaction of agitation.

In any case, we returned to our normal operations. There were many successful operations handled by the brigade today. An enemy anti-tank team was neutralized. Some soldiers identified terrorists firing at them, so they retaliated and eliminated them. Later, they discovered a locked area, opened it with an explosive charge, and found a terrorist killed by the blast, with a Golani Brigade flag and a sergeant's crate next to him. Other companies also identified and eliminated more terrorists. The snipers from our original company (Ladany, Shtrull, Yagur, Shlomi, and Brown) took down 4 terrorists at the school west of the Indonesian hospital. I remember that there were a few more successful encounters, but I don't quite recall all the details.

Before we went to sleep, we had various interesting discussions within the team, such as education in the secular population versus the religious one, and more. It was nice to have diverse topics of conversation. We went to sleep. Throughout the night, the Air Force didn't stop bombing southwards of us, and our building shook all night long. In addition to our forces' fire, there were several hours when mortar fire was directed towards us. I started to appreciate the sound of a mortar in flight, especially the sound of the illuminating mortar rounds. It's a kind of deep and ominous sound that strengthens as the mortar gets closer to you. If I were to try to compare the sound to something, I would say it's like an echoing ripple of waves. During my last guard duty for the night, we were informed there was suspicious movement at the mosque. I tried to see from our position if I could spot anything, but it was extremely foggy, and I could barely see beyond 50 meters in front of me, even with the night-vision goggles. I went to sleep.

Tuesday, December 5, 2023

04:30 – Shlomi and Amitai leave together with the sniper team of the supporting forces for an ambush on the Lima-Edel axis.

At 07:30, they reported identifying a terrorist leaving the mosque area. The Benny team quickly encircled him, and Shitrit the Negevist of the team took up position and neutralized the terrorist. They then went into cover and circled him, threw a grenade and Shmuel confirmed that he was neutralized.

The terrorist was an oversized young man, and upon searching him, they found a large combat knife. The encounter was just 50 meters away from us, but while the

Benny team was busy eliminating the terrorist, we were busy with our morning routine – coffee and a briefing from Nahman.

At around 09:30, Jake went for a briefing with the battalion commander, and then we received an order: the company is to scan for Hamas operatives located north of us. The Snippe team leads, Jake's operations command team in the center, and Nahman's team at the rear. Meir, the force build-up officer of the team, informs us that Oz and I will stay behind to guard. That sucks! There's a sense that the upcoming operation is going to be interesting. Yemini says to me, "Kuno, get ready, it's going to be crazy." I nod while being disappointed that I'm not going with them.

The team heads toward the buildings. Five minutes into guard duty, a strong explosion is heard from the direction the teams had left. Shit! It's really close. There are certainly injuries among our forces. I shift my gaze from the position and identify a large smoke cloud. In the background I hear shouts, "They stepped on an explosive." Oz rushes into the room, and we both look at each other. The same thought passes through both of our minds. I hope no one is hurt. The team leader reports, "I have two lightly injured soldiers in the force." We check everyone is present and okay. Aside from the wounded in the Snippe team, all forces are okay.

I hear Nahman calling Kaneti to tend to the wounded. It's good to hear the Snippe team and Nahman in communication, transmitting calmness and proper battle management. Suddenly, two more explosions are heard from the northeast. I identify from the sound that it's a detonation charge, but quite far from our forces. The explosion occurs in the northern school building, situated in the Rothman sector. We understand it's a remotely-triggered charge – i.e. a Hamas observer is looking at us.

We try to identify him but to no avail, the combat medic is called in to treat the wounded. Everything is conducted by the book. It's very relieving to hear that nobody was seriously injured. It was a major miracle. Just before the charge exploded, Oz was playing with my GoPro and it turns out he accidentally started recording a video, so we now have documentation of the event. We can't see anything in the footage, but we can hear the radio communications.

The team heads back, the Benny team leaves an ambush and a lookout, hoping to find the observer who triggered the charge. The team returns sweaty, and Nahman sums up the activities. Eden Azulay, who was injured, suddenly enters, and the whole team applauds our battle-wounded comrade. He got hit by shrapnel in his right hand, but after he was given painkillers, he seemed fine.

Eden enthusiastically recounts the miracle they experienced and waits for his evacuation. He jokes, "I got myself a great 'Panorama'" (a well-known combo of the words "referral" and "shawarma") and the guys laugh. A bunch of the guys from the Snippe team were hit by shrapnel and bits that flew during the explosion, but Eden was the only one who was seriously injured. It turns out one of the guys accidentally filmed the actual explosion. Eden shows us the video – it's truly insane. You see the Snippe team advancing, and suddenly they get "swallowed" into a ball of fire, with a mushroom cloud of smoke rising over it – with the team inside. It's not every day that you manage to document such an event.

When I spoke with Kaneti after the conversation with Eden, I asked how he felt when Nahman called him to treat the wounded. He replied that before he saw the severity of the injury, he was sure he would be dealing with all kinds of serious injuries like limb amputations and more. No doubt the run towards the scene was a scary moment. However, he took a deep breath, mentally went through the procedures for dealing with the wounded, and ran.

We very quickly return to routine. Playing, talking. Victor and Meir prepared an elaborate lunch.

Shlomi and Amitai return from the sniper ambush. They did an excellent job today as well. It turns out that earlier in the morning, Eldar, the sniper team commander of the auxiliary force, identified a terrorist with a weapon advancing towards the junction. Bar, the spotter, directed Sasson towards the terrorist, and they eliminated him.

Later on, they saw a guy moving suspiciously with a wheelchair, surrounded by five other guys at a distance of 720 meters. Suddenly, the guy stops, and the group around him assists in setting up a rocket launcher. A precise shot from Amitai – and the party over there ends. It drives me crazy, once again, to hear how the enemy forces us to be suspicious of every "humanitarian" case, like a disabled person. The real losers are the truly disabled in Gaza, whom we have no choice but to assume are playing us. Two minutes later, the snipers identify rocket launches at very close range to the position the terrorists tried to set up. Apparently, there was an attempt to execute launches from multiple positions simultaneously, but Shlomi, Amitai, and the sniper team managed to prevent the setting up of at least one of the positions. Half an hour later, a group of teenagers try to approach the wheelchair and rocket launching position. The sniper team, together with Shlomi and Amitai, identifies another terrorist riding fast on a bike and attempting to reach the position, but with sharp identification from the spotters and quick direction from the snipers, the terrorist falls on his side. Within ten seconds, his friends drag the body away. It turns out the snipers of the 9th Company had a successful day and took down several terrorists. In hindsight, we realize that the terrorist we identified in the morning, leaving the mosque area, is likely the one who placed the detonated charge on the Snippe team. It's not confirmed, but that's our assumption.

So, time passes, and we prepare for an order to occupy a new complex, south of the Adel axis.

The platoon's mission is to capture the mosque and "Bonbon Halls" in order to observe the Indonesian Hospital, as there is suspicion that Hamas is hiding missing (kidnapped) bodies there. The goal: to allow the Shayetet (an elite commando force) to sweep the compound and to open the Greenland axis for secure truck movement. Ultimately, this will enable IDF soldiers to load bodies onto refrigerated trucks so that they can be brought to Israel to determine if they are one of the kidnapped Israelis. We need to start attacking the targets within an hour of receiving the alert order from the Shayetet.

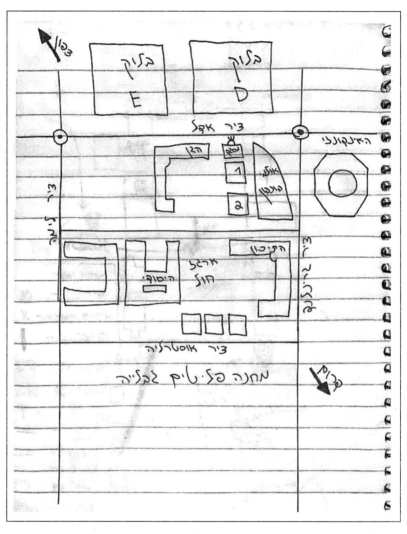

The school compound in Jabaliya and the Indonesian Hospital[30]

---

30 This drawing depicts the school compound (represented by the shapes and rectangles in the middle of the page), as well as the Indonesia Hospital (the octagon and circle on the right side).

The night passes, and there is still no alert order. Just before we decide to go to sleep, the Battalion Commander arrives for a discussion with the team. He talks about the missions ahead and his expectations from us, and he concludes by saying that he greatly appreciates us and what we are doing. It was a good conversation. We go to sleep, ready for an emergency wake-up.

Wednesday, December 6, 2023

We get woken up at 05:00. The Shayetet swept the hospital compound and didn't find any bodies there. We canceled the attack. We all felt a twinge in our hearts. The thought that families are still waiting for any news from their loved ones and haven't received, continues to haunt us. We hoped we could at least help give some of these families closure.

The Nahman Team went out at 05:15 for a planned operation on a building where we suspected the observer from yesterday was staying. Eight of us went from the team, while the rest stayed behind to sleep. It's amazing to see how much the explosion incident impacted us. We're all hyper-alert. Peak combat routine performance. Manoeuvering as needed, with coverings, ear plugs, and goggles. Distance between each person. For the sake of fairness, I'll mention that the team's overall level of combat performance is very high, both generally and compared to other teams, but we were being particularly rigorous now.

As we stand in front of the target, Oz and Michali "raise the grenade launcher" and launch 5 grenades into the building. Kashi launches a LAW into the building. If there was someone inside the building, there probably isn't much left of them.

Heavy rain starts to fall and we begin to head back towards the stronghold. We return to the stronghold wet and satisfied, the deputy company commander of the supporting force adds that he is also proud of us, and pleased to see the team's professionalism. Nahman sums up the initiative and from there, we go up to the stronghold.

Some of us are going back to sleep, while some are already starting the day. I'm taking advantage of the time to write. When everyone is up, we listen to Nahman's briefing and then get the site organized.

At 10:00, Jake arrives to deliver a new order. The battalion's mission: capture a nearby block and gain operational control of the Lima-Adel-Greenland intersections. Jake asked if anyone wanted to make a call or send a message over the Red Phone. I immediately jumped at the opportunity. I had assured Shiran that during this outing, I would try to stay more in touch. Amsterdam responded, and I know that he and Shiran are good friends, and it comforts me knowing that Shiran has friends around her. Shiran tells me that she worries about me but mainly misses me, it's hard for her, but she manages to cope.

Before entering Gaza, Shiran asked me to recite a chapter of Psalms every day, and I told her I would try. The thing is I didn't know it by heart, so I didn't always manage to say it. But during the last outing, Shiran wrote a letter and added the chapter at the end so that I remember it (she's the best), and since then, I've recited it every day. Today, I had the chance to say it together with Shiran on the Red Phone.

I finished the conversation and returned for Jake's order. I was hungry and thirsty. I shoved the garlic bread with tahini and tuna that I had just made into my mouth. Nahman, Suedi and I go over all the details down to the team-level. It's a building similar to the one we are in now, and we decide to try to breach the northern wall of the building and enter it from an unexpected direction so that if they decide to detonate the entrance, the explosives won't be directed towards us. It also allows us to open fire towards the advancing direction. If we fail to breach, the Spear Squad will enter through the main door after throwing grenades at the entrance, hoping to initiate the detonators and sever the cables that activate them.

Following the Spear, Squad B will enter, scanning the ground floor while Squad C stops on the basement floor (-1), so we'll slowly scan all the floors. Like clockwork – one squad scans, another follows, and the third secures the staircase. Once we finish scanning a floor, the team that secured the staircase leads the scan on the next floor. In this way, we plan on "washing" the combat up to the 5th floor, clearing the building of people and explosives.

We are preparing to leave the stronghold that has served us for the last three days. We are all organizing our personal and team equipment. "12:30, exit!" announces Nahman. Yemini and I – the team members who are in charge of explosives – realize we have less than an hour to pack our bags, create an improvised breach frame (since we ran out of frames), and manage to conduct a frame deployment exercise if we have any time left.

At 12:15, we quickly grab our bags and head out. On the way, Meir identifies an iron cover inside a concrete frame that might be used as a tunnel entrance. We request immediate approval from the battalion commander, who is standing next to us, to open the cover and rule out the possibility that it's a tunnel shaft. I pull out a rope anchor from the bag, Nahman connects the anchor to the cover, and I lay out the rope. Everyone finds cover. I declare loudly, "Explosion ready" and count backwards 3... 2... 1..., pulling the rope firmly backward, feeling and hearing the cover open. Nahman and Meir cautiously approach the pit and discover a waterproof watch, nothing special. I quickly fold the rope and anchor, shoving it into the bag.

For the first time during this outing in Gaza we meet the Kesten Team. They say during this platoon isn't the same without us and that they miss us. While we talk, the building next to us goes up in flames. The 9th Company burned down the building they were in. It's nice to see the guys from the 9th after a long time without seeing each other.

We chat with them briefly while the Snippe team and the Benny team start to take control of the area we are supposed to enter. As soon as they finish the mission, we move towards their building ready to breach the wall. Once we receive confirmation, we run – me, Yemini and the Spear – to the site. We notice that in addition to the concrete coating, there is also a Jerusalem stone coating, so the chances of the IED successfully making a hole in the wall are low. We decide to place it anyway. We search for the most sensitive point on the wall and set the charge. Yemini connects the detonator and winds the Nonel (shock tube detonator) back. The moment we receive clearance, we count backward on the radio, "Proper explosion in 7... 4... 2... 1... boom."

Nahman shouts an order to charge and enter the battle. We all run forward, ready to sweep and take over the building. Dotan throws a smoke grenade to hide us as we enter the battle. We reach the northern wall of the building and see that the charge has made a nice neat hole in the building, but there are still some iron bars blocking the passage. Nahman goes straight to plan B – entering through the front door with grenades and heavy fire. Yemini and I go back to Squad C and suddenly I notice 20 soldiers running like crazy towards me with a bewildered look in their eyes.

"Where was the explosion? Where are the wounded?" For a moment, I don't understand what they're talking about. It's Benyamini, along with the medical corps of the 9th Company, the medical corps of the auxiliary team, and other attachments. They're all running towards us. It turns out that after we blew up the frame, they heard us shouting and returning on Nahman's orders, and they were freaking out. I saunter towards them, "What happened? Are we not supposed to fight with some fervor?" What can I say, not everyone is used to the Nahman team's strength. We made sure to update on both the company and battalion radios about the explosion.

It seems like all the medics and medical corps who rushed to the event still had their pulses racing, but we were less concerned. We started "washing the battle."

Shaked and Dotan lead. Nahman and Michaeli follow them, just like in the plan. Shaked slides a grenade to the door and counts backward, **explosion!** Grenades have a certain disadvantage in battle, as after you throw a grenade, it takes time for the dust to settle, which slightly delays the fight. We wait. It's not that it's suddenly pleasant to breathe, rather suffocating in a way that still allows us to breathe.

As we planned, we scan and clear the building. "Yemini and Kuno to me," Nahman announces. Yemini and I smile. I tell him, "Yemini, get the explosive ready." The door is a classic steel door that's locked. Very quickly we attach the explosives to the handle and tie them together with a detonating cord.

We tie a combat activation device to the detonating cord, ignite the fuse with a lighter, count backwards. I activate a stopper. According to my calculation, we have 1:06 minutes until the explosion. "Proper explosion in 3... 2... 1...," **boom**.

I was pleased to know that I was precise with the timings, and we continued. At the end of the mission, Yemini and I finished with a total of 8 doors blown up. It was really good. Both of us feel that our teamwork significantly improved. Less talk, more understanding, one glance from Yemini and I know exactly what he wants.

We finished taking control of and clearing the building. We found combat equipment and Hamas flags inside. Like in every Gaza operation, this site is full of pictures of martyrs. We quickly start building our stronghold. On the fifth floor, the company's snipers are located together with the remote command center. We position ourselves on the fourth floor. The whole team is doing exceptional work.

Yemini and I climb to the snipers to create firing holes with explosives. We are actually right next to the school; a hundred meters from us there are hundreds of civilians and terrorists. What a horrific situation. This morning, the 7008th Battalion identified a terrorist executing a Gazan child who attempted to escape from the school. Hamas is aware that we do not attack schools because of the civilians inside, so they place guards at the entrances. Anyone who tries to escape is executed. Hamas kills "its" people, and the world remains silent. Only when we defend ourselves, the UN suddenly wakes up and condemns us. It's an upside-down world.

Very quickly, all the chaos of the stronghold is transformed into a home. Some of us clean the floor, arranging a huge lounge for the team with couches we take from the lower apartments. The others seal the windows and set up positions. Yemini and I put up corrugated metal for soundproofing at the entrance of the building, and then the bathroom. After an hour and a half of intense teamwork, we possess a very high-quality stronghold. Oz managed to connect lighting and Suedi hung the Israeli flag in the lounge. Towards the evening, Nahman gave a briefing on the positions, neighboring forces' locations, and events that occurred today in our zone. We were completely exhausted. Victor and Meir prepared dinner, but I went to sleep.

They woke me up for guard duty at 23:00 with Yemini. There had been a resupply while I was sleeping. The guard duty passed really quickly. Yemini was on duty with me and we shared a really good conversation. During the shift a donkey passed and made noises, and every time it moved, we had to pointlessly check. For the next guard duty, I got up with Suedi. I made sweet tea for us, and the shift went well. After that, we went to sleep.

Thursday, First Night of Hanukkah, December 7, 2023

We woke up to a relatively calm morning. I had another guard shift in the early morning and I stayed awake. I used the time for writing, prayers, and thoughts. There were sounds of explosions and gunfire outside, nothing unusual.

Nothing unusual except for the excavator that worked at a fast pace, Up until yesterday it stood between us and the Adel-Mall Axis, but not anymore. At night, when we discussed possible threats to our outpost, one of the main threats was a terrorist infiltrating through the Adel Axis or Lima Axis under the cover of the mall, for the simple reason that we had no way of completely preventing passage there. These tools have so much power, it's insane. Within a few hours, the mall was turned into a pile of rubble quickly flattened by the crawl of the diggers and tractors. An ancient saying goes, "There are three things a person can watch without getting tired: flowing water, a burning fire, and another person working." I don't know which category the D9 diggers fall under, but I can assure you that you can watch them for hours while they destroy buildings.

At the same time, the snipers identified a large man in a leather jacket standing at the entrance to an elementary school with a notebook in hand, writing all sorts of things, while preventing civilians from leaving. Another man was there helping him.

The snipers waited for the right opportunity, when both men would be standing outside, so they could take the men out together. Meanwhile, the snipers received an update through their radios that troops would soon start to make announcements toward the school and begin to approach it, in an effort to encourage the civilians to flee the site. At around 10:30, I hear our announcement in Arabic telling the civilians to leave the school, so that they don't get hurt in the mission. Our snipers had a problem: he was always surrounding himself with women and children. Clearly, he was aware that we wanted to eliminate him.

Later on, when I spoke with one of the snipers, he told me that the terrorist had gone up to the roof and faced us, holding a baby to protect himself. The baby belonged to one of the women who surrounded him. The terrorist knew that the baby would provide him with the best cover he could ask for – our morality. The uncompromising and unequivocal morality of the IDF. Behind him there was no friend he wanted to protect in the name of friendship and camaraderie, just a scared photographer trying to catch the moment when the "occupation army" shoots an innocent baby. But we're better than that.

On one occasion, he goes out to the balcony surrounded by women and children. One of the women moved ever so slightly to the side, but that was enough for our snipers.

Sasson pulls the trigger and the terrorist falls. In one brief moment the whole situation changes. The women and children start screaming, and the terrorists who were behind them take him, and within a few seconds, lay him on a door that they use as a stretcher. It was swift and impressive. They seem to be used to this already. In the background, an announcement in Arabic calls again for civilians to leave the area around the school. The announcements, along with the killing of the guard, prompts a swarm of civilians to start to leave.

Those civilians are in a terrible situation. But – and it's a big but – there's an attempt to create the sense that these are innocent civilians. That's not really the case, at least not for many of them. It's true that they are currently at war and that Hamas uses them as human shields, but until two months ago many of them are the very same people who were proud of their "martyrs" and hung up flags in their homes of Hamas, Palestinian Islamic Jihad and other organizations whose goals are to destroy the Jewish people and the "Zionist enemy". I know because I've been inside their homes. These are the same people who called their murderous children on October 7th and told them that they were proud of them. These are the people to whom we give shelter and humanitarian aid. Though this makes me feel uneasy, I understand and I am glad that we maintain our status as an army proud of its values and morality.

As everyone was fleeing outside, Shmuel, from the Benny team, identified a terrorist fleeing under civilian cover and shot towards him. Everything calms down. A lull on the radio, no sounds of gunshots. We settle down to eat and talk.

Another big explosion. We don't give it much notice; after all, explosions have become a routine thing.

I see Michaeli holding two radios and trying to understand what's happening. In his right hand is the radio tuned to the battalion frequency, and in his left hand is the one tuned to the company frequency. With all the chatter on the radio, I can't understand anything, but it seems like Michaeli somehow manages to follow. I pick up words like "charge," "injured," and "urgently evacuate." Shit. I hope everyone is okay, even though it sounds bad. I reassure myself that when the Snippe team evacuated due to an explosive going off it sounded bad at first, but in the end, it turned out less worrying. But there's another voice inside me saying, "Miracles don't happen twice." I hope I'm wrong. I'm tired of hearing stories on the news about wonderful boys, full of innocence and beauty. I'm sick of it. I don't want to hear stories of heroism and camaraderie. I want to hear that the South Ayalon Highway is full of traffic up to the La Guardia Interchange. That Maccabi Tel Aviv won yesterday, 2-1. I wish! I wish all this hadn't happened.

I divert my thoughts and continue to mess around and talk to my friends as if nothing happened, until it's announced over the radio that we have two seriously injured soldiers being airlifted. Enough! A helicopter evacuation in battle is a bad sign. It means there's no time, and they prefer to put the helicopter in danger. I try to understand where the charge exploded. It turns out it was at the same spot where it exploded on the Snippe team. How shitty. Are we really falling at the same spot twice? Rumors begin to circulate that there's a "pursuit" of the force. I ignore it and return to the regular conversation. There's a voice in me that says that if I think too much about what's happening here, I'll be a less good soldier. There's a time to fight and a time to process. Now it's time to fight.

But we're not doing much. When we took control of the site that we're currently in, it was the most critical point of friction in the battalion, but now the 98th Division has bypassed us from the south and captured the school area, and other units have also become the front line. Our zone is relatively calm. While the 98th Division and the Multi-Dimensional Unit are fighting, the 9th and 10th Companies – the ones which had the charge go off – fight to the north of us, near the Lima Axis. There's intelligence about a suspicious tunnel inside a concrete factory, but to understand the significance of this tunnel, some more details are needed.

When we entered Jabaliya, we were informed that the Air Force had killed Hamas's North Brigade Commander. We didn't know where it happened, but we were just happy that we had advanced another step in destroying Hamas. We were also informed that during the ceasefire, Hamas had re-dug the collapsed tunnel in which the brigade commander was killed, and found his body. Three Israeli hostages were found dead in that tunnel. Hamas claimed that they were killed by an IDF bomb, but the IDF informed the families that it couldn't be determined how the hostages were killed, and they likely did not die as a result of a bombing or shooting. I don't know what happened, but with every such story, my heart sinks even more. We are here giving our all to find the hostages and bring them back. What a terrible situation.

160 meters from the area that we're in, is the house of

the Hamas North Brigade Commander. The intelligence we received links the tunnel in the concrete factory to the commander's house, and presumably to the location of the body. We still don't know exactly where the tunnel in the concrete factory is, and that's where the teams were headed. On the way there, they passed by the tunnel where the Snippe team's charge was activated, and... they also activated the explosives themselves. Apparently, simultaneously, two IEDs were set off on them—one near the tunnel and one inside it. When they passed by, they identified a double-wired cable. Normally, this should raise suspicion of an IED, but they thought it was remnants from the Snippe team's one and therefore didn't lend much importance to it. Later on, the Betzel team informed us that they had sat near the tunnel half an hour before it had exploded, and everything seemed normal to them. After the explosion, the companies continued fighting and scanning the concrete factory.

Tonight will be the first night of Hanukkah. When we entered Gaza, I was sure we would be out by the first night, at least that's what the brigade commander said. But lately, it seems like the times and the brigade commander aren't aligning.

I think a lot about Shiranush and hope she's alright. It's getting a bit tough for me. I miss her a lot. I was delighted that I managed to ask my mom before we entered, to send Shiran a letter and flowers in case I don't make it for the holiday. I took the time to write a few words to Shiran. Later I tried to call her on the Red Phone, but unfortunately, she didn't answer. Jake's sister, who serves in the reserves as well, also has a Red Phone, so I sent her a picture of the letter in the hope that she could pass it on to Shiran.

We had a team candle-lighting ceremony at the stronghold; Nahman said a few words, and we sang "Ma'oz Tzur"[31] together. It was emotional. I also lit some candles alone and thought about us, my dear Shiran; about me and you, especially about you. I imagined you standing next to me here, and it filled me with joy. I asked Meir to take a picture of me during the lighting, so at least we'll have a nice momento.

In the evening, we received the bitter news: there were indeed fatalities. Gal Eisenkot and Eyal Berkowitz fell in battle. Such pain. There's a rumor that when they made the announcement about the explosion and Gal's injury, Gadi Eisenkot[32] was in the Division's command center and heard about it over the radio. Truly heartbreaking. I didn't know them personally, but they were from my battalion, and it hits close to home. When Nahman informed us of their deaths, we were in the middle of eating. "They fell in battle," he said. "Take some time to process this." At that moment, it hit me like thunder, I couldn't eat anymore. A severe nausea overwhelmed me. I didn't know how to cope with it, just like I don't know now how to handle it. So, I did what I excelled at recently: deny. Not think about it, as if nothing had happened. I don't know how it is in real life, but here it's proving effective. They say it might explode in the end, but for now, it's the only solution I see.

After taking a few minutes to digest the painful

31 A traditional Hanukkah song.
32 Gal's father, and former Chief of Staff of the IDF.

event, Nahman gave us a night briefing. This time, he mainly focused on the changes to the borders of our zone and the shooting directions due to movements of forces in the area. We finished the briefing and I went to sleep relatively early. It took me a long time to fall asleep, and then I was already woken up to do guard duty.

At around 21:00 we received supplies: there was water, food, and burgers. But what made me most happy were the letters! Shiran made sure to send me letters from Dad, Mom, Tzion, Tchelet, and of course, from her. As I read them, tears filled my eyes. Suddenly, it flooded me with longing for home, for family, for my wife. I am so proud of my family and my wife.

Friday, Second Night of Hanukkah, December 8, 2023

I finished my last shift at 05:00 and stayed up to write until all the guys woke up at 08:30. There were crazy sounds of explosions. I've never heard bombs in such large quantities. The Air Force, along with artillery and mortars, went on for an hour non-stop.

I remembered that during one of the guard shifts we were informed on the radio that the Benda team, the one who stepped on the IED yesterday, was leaving for funerals and returning immediately afterwards to combat. When I poked my head out the window, all of Jabaliya was covered in smoke. Suddenly there was gunfire towards us; it sounded like the burst of a Kalashnikov. I got up from the sofa which was exposed to the window and moved to the other side and I continued writing. Snippe reported over the radio, "We identified gunshots towards us," but it didn't excite me. There were always shootings and bombings here.

We are protected from direct fire because the 98th Division is between us and the area from which the shooting was carried out. So writing feels like a good response to me. Later, I approached one of the walls in the building and retrieved bullets that hit it, as a memento.

In this way, another day passed. In our stronghold it's relatively calm and quiet. The 9th and 10th Companies continue to fight and sweep the area near the concrete factory. It turns out that the Feuer team found a building next to the concrete factory with a large amount of ready-to-use IEDs. In addition, there is a 30 meter deep tunnel with an elevator inside, in the zone of the Reconnaissance team.

The Kesten team, which went past the tunnel which was blown up by the Snippe and Benda teams, found another charge that terrorists had placed during the night. Of course, they neutralized it. During the day, they brought a D9 to collapse the tunnel shaft. There's always a dilemma about what to do with tunnels: on one hand, you can investigate them to understand the tunnel route, on the other hand, there is a desire to destroy them so that the terrorists cannot use them. The brigade understood that this tunnel was less relevant and chose to collapse it, unlike the reconnaissance team's tunnel, which they chose to investigate.

The team wakes up, and Nahman gives a morning briefing: "We need two volunteers to assist the Atzitz team with guard shifts." Suedi and I volunteer, after we tidy up the house and I pray quickly. I take a bag with me, with my pen and notebook, medical supplies, and caffeine pills. Of course, we're in full combat gear. We go down the stairs of our building to the ground floor, and then I shout to the soldier manning the radio to make sure the forces in the zone know that we are entering the Atziz team's building. He shouts back, "They know!" I ask in response, "Suedi, are you ready?" "Ready for what?" he asks me. Instead of answering him, I announce and shout in a loud voice, "Kuno and Suedi are maneuvering." I then pat Suedi on the back with a smile and a small wink, and start running towards the Atzitz team's building. Suedi runs after me, one hand on the weapon, the other on the bag and softshell jacket, and his head moves from side to side. Only those who know Suedi will understand what I mean when I say that his head bobs when he runs.

We arrive at the building. Atzitz is waiting for us downstairs. "Wow, Kuno and Suedi, we got the best of Nahman's team," he smiles. Then he adds, "When we heard that your team was sending two comrades to reinforce us, we knew straight away that it would be you who came." I was happy to see them. The Atzitz team are really good guys. There were a total of six guys from the Atzitz team there, because the rest of the company were on missions around the factory.

Our mission is to protect the battalion's stronghold. There are two positions, so we each take every third shift. It's not a great ratio, but not terrible either. When we arrived, Nitai and Helman gave us a tour to understand the positions.

Afterwards, we prepared a breakfast for ourselves: cucumber and tomato salad with corn, tahini, tuna and garlic. No complaints. Overall, we live well. I'm on the radio, Suedi is at the other position. After half an hour, we switch.

While on duty, I start running through various scenarios in my head, and I realize that this is a relatively exposed position. If a terrorist were to arrive, he could surprise me and I would find myself at a tactical disadvantage. I took a grenade from the vest and held it in my hand during the shift, so that if a terrorist tried to surprise me, even before he realized what was happening, he'd be hit with a grenade.

I was satisfied with my solution. I was sitting on a chair with a small table in front of me, my notebook and a cup of tea placed on it. Suddenly, I heard bursts of gunfire towards me. In less than a second, I jumped down from the chair and stood behind the curtain next to the window sill. My right hand gripping the grenade and my left hand clutching the pin, ready for any scenario. Very quickly, I realized that it was a mistaken identification and that it was a nearby firing of our forces towards the enemy.

I sat back down and discovered that aside from an injury by the enemy's gunfire, the very worst thing had happened: the notebook which I had worked so hard to write and describe everything that we've gone through was completely soaked. As I jumped from the chair, the tea cup on the table had spilled onto the notebook. It seems this is one scenario I didn't consider. Within a second, I picked up the notebook, grabbed a pack of tissues, separated the pages, and placed tissues between each page. Then I fanned out all the pages with block fragments to dry them. Luckily, it was a sunny day. I placed the notebook in the sun and I spent 4 hours drying it and praying that it wouldn't be ruined. After 4 intense hours, in which I flipped every page, dried them with tissues and in the sun, and repeated carefully, the notebook returned to itself. I tell myself that I have to finish with this notebook, wrap it in plastic, and send it out of Gaza so that nothing happens to it.

It's a nice coincidence that as I write about this event, I'm actually on the last page of the notebook. Today is Friday, and because I was busy with the notebook, I didn't notice the time. During the time left between the shifts, I prepare IEDs with the demolition blocks and the detonating cord I have. From my point of view, the goal is to have everything ready in advance: the detonation bag, a C explosive, a C4 explosive, explosive blocks of various sizes as needed, already connected to the detonating cord. All of this is so that at the time of need, I can load anything I want in minimal time.

Third Notebook

Continuation

Later, I heard on the radio that two guys from the Benny team spotted a black car emerging from the direction of the school. From the way it was driven, it seems it felt threatened by our sniper position, but that didn't really help it, because our snipers made sure it no longer posed a threat.

While I was busy preparing some charges, someone asked, "Who wants to join me in lighting Hanukkah candles?" What? Candle lighting already? That means Shabbat is almost starting. There were so many things I wanted to finish before Shabbat. I folded everything up and prepared myself for lighting the candles.

I didn't notice who offered to light with us nor did I recognize his voice. I asked Avni, a good guy from the Atzitz team, and he told me that it was a guy from the battalion remote command center. I went up to the command center and saw a guy named Yosef, dressed in green military pants and a white shirt, wrapped in a tallit,[33] arranging the candles. He had an ornate menorah, wicks, and olive oil. It moved me. I managed to close my eyes and imagined myself with Shiran and the family lighting candles. Soon after, Yosef also arranged a menorah for me. Just

---

33 Prayer shawl.

before sunset, we made sure to darken the stronghold with blankets and nails. It's not typical to see a guy wrapped in a tallit, hammering nails and hanging blankets in the middle of a warzone. It looked like something out of a movie.

After we finished sealing the apartment and the building's staircase, I sat down with Nir, "the screwdriver," the operations officer of the battalion, and asked him to explain the situation of our forces. It was nice to look at the layout and understand the Gaza Strip more.

The Strip is divided into three parts: north, center, and south. In the north, battles are taking place in Jabaliya, Gaza City, and Saja'iyya, while all other areas are under our control. In the south, the 98th Division is engaged in battles in Khan Yunis, and in the center, they are fighting in Deir al-Balah. I asked Nir if he knew about the two explosions that occurred northeast of the school, which occurred at the same time as an explosion on the Snippe team. He said no. I shared the locations of the explosions with him because I thought it might affect our understanding of the tunnel layout in the area.

I remembered that when we were in Beit Hanoun, we found a map in one of the trucks that took part in the October 7th Hamas massacre. That map, apparently, was also used for a Hamas military drill. It marked, among other things, arrows signifying the advancement of their forces, names of Israeli towns, and breach points on the border. After we found the map, just before we sent it back to Israel, we tried to compare it to the map on the "switchblade" (location response device) and noticed that the entire drill took place in the Gaza Strip:

the exercise began in the northern area of the Strip (where the town of Dugit once was) and advanced southeast to the breach point.

We did indeed find a Hamas training facility in one of the blocks we captured. Inside this training facility was a one-to-one model of the wall at the Erez border crossing: a concrete wall made of concrete cylinders, a meter wide and about ten meters high, positioned side by side. I told Nir about it.

Yosef suggested that we pray the Shabbat evening services together. I went down to update Suedi, and he joined me. We talked about all the places we had been: Beit Hanoun, Beit Lahiya, Al-Atatra ridge, Jabaliya. Yosef decided to give each place a Jewish name. He told us, "Initially we were at El-Hanun and then moved to Bet Leah. We had a defense battle in Bet Atara and now we are conquering Galia." There was something amusing about the naturalness with which he spoke about it. He then gave a short sermon in honor of Hanukkah, and of course, he made a connection between us and the Maccabees. I write "of course" because all of us feel a connection between the story of the Maccabees and our war against Hamas. A war of light against darkness, good against evil.

The guys from the command center invited us to a Shabbat dinner. It was insane. They laid a Shabbat table with dishes, cutlery, glasses, napkins, and soup bowls. It turns out that Yosef is the cook for the battalion command center. We said Kiddush over Cabernet Sauvignon wine, which he made sure to bring from home (in an orange juice bottle). We said the "HaMotzi" blessing over the rolls. Then he brought out everything he cooked: warm hummus with parsley, rice with fried sausages, and barley soup. On the table were fizzy and sweet drinks. In short, it was a true Shabbat-like experience.

However, it very much triggered my homesickness, and I missed Shiran. Of course, the food can't compare to home cooking, but in the current situation, it was very good, even excellent. I ate quickly because I needed to go downstairs and start my guard shift. When I finished my shift, four guys from the Eshel team arrived. They had returned from an ambush nearby the concrete factory along with all the crew's LAW bags. The decision was made that the Eshel team would return to the stronghold so that we could handle all the tasks and maintain the stronghold during the night. They arrived hungry and tired. Truth be told, it feels like the 9th Company has been working very hard these past two days. After they had the chance to eat from Yosef's table and brought their bags up to the site, we sat down to talk.

I enjoyed talking with them. They're great guys. I told them that I had "bad-mouthed" them a bit in my notebook, and they laughed about it. We had a good conversation. The Eshel team is very young. They had recently been discharged from their mandatory service, and almost all of them came to the war straight from their post-army trip abroad, often cutting it short, which I think is commendable. In addition, their reserve commander is the same commander they had during basic and advanced training. In my opinion, the continuation of relationships they had during their training period makes up for their youth. We talked to them about the importance of speaking directly and openly with the team commander. It's important to know when to "turn it on" and maintain operational alertness and when to relax and let go. Ultimately, if you're always trying to keep up operational alertness, it actually causes awareness to drop at times when it's needed.

It seems that the Hamas commander of the Northern Brigade has more than one house, because it turns out that while we were with the auxiliary company, the 9th Company went to sweep another house associated with the Northern Brigade commander, in Block D, and found many interesting things. An Iranian-made rifle, gun magazines, an advanced night vision device which we have yet to encounter in Gaza, and also – Hitler's book, "Mein Kampf," translated into Arabic, along with many other documents from the Erez Crossing. It's no exaggeration to call them the Nazis of our times. It seems that during their raid on October 7th, they took everything they could. In the house we found IDF operation books, a notebook belonging to one of the soldiers, logbooks describing the logistics routines of the base, professional literature, event investigations, and even an "exemption from shaving" letter of one of the soldiers.

We finished our conversation, said goodbye to the Atzitz, Eshel and remote command center teams, and returned to our team after a whole day away from them.

Shabbat, Third Night of Hanukkah, December 9, 2023

There's something about Shabbat during wartime that's extremely challenging, especially when we aren't on the front lines and are mostly waiting. Time passes slowly. At least for me, there's no sense of rest. On the contrary – even when I'm sitting idly and there apparently isn't much to do, feelings of stress and intranquility arise and intensify. There's something in me that really wants Shabbat to end.

We try to pass the time with games, naps, guard shifts, or simply eating, but nothing helps. In the morning, Dotan said Kiddush, and since then, Shabbat has just dragged on. Outside, there's a lot of shooting and bombings, but here in the stronghold, it's relatively calm. There's chaos over the radio, especially on the brigade's frequency. In all honesty, I didn't have the energy to follow everything that was happening on the radio. I told myself I would wait until 21:00 for the brigade-wide situational assessment, then I could hear everything in an organized manner.

This idleness is affecting us all. The guys start talking about how they need to be at home, and how dejected we are. In my opinion, there's a sort of bell curve – inactivity does indeed lead to the erosion of strength, but too much activity also provokes the same. We need to try to find the balance somewhere in the middle.

Over Shabbat, there was talk about a precise mortar fire called "Purple Rain" toward the 98th Division. There are rumors that they have casualties. There was also anti-tank fire on tanks. As I said, I was waiting for the brigade-wide assessment.

Sunset, darkness started to fall, and as usual, we hung blankets on the windows to obscure our location and prepare for the night. The religious among us recited the evening prayers and right after, Meir led Havdallah for the team. We organized the stronghold and lit Hanukkah candles together. Dotan lit them, and everyone responded with "A-a-amen" in the familiar tune.

After we finished everything, Meir prepared a guard duty list. I took the first guard shift while several team members went to fetch supplies. Victor prepared a delicious lentil soup. Later, I took the Red Phone from one of Jake's soldiers and called Shiran. I was so emotional when she answered the phone, and so was Shiran. She had just started to share about how tough it's been for her, and then the call disconnected. No reception. For half an hour, I tried to call, attempting to move between rooms without any success. What a bummer. I think about Shiran. It must be so hard for her. I promise myself that I'll try to catch her again in the morning.

At 21:00 I finished guard duty just as the brigade-wide situational assessment began. The 98th Division received targeted drone or mortar fire on their forces, resulting in five injuries. They captured the school, eliminated 19 terrorists, found a Go-Pro camera with videos of Hamas training, and also discovered a lot of weapons, mostly guns and grenades.

Sultan (the multidimensional unit) found vests, nine Kalashnikov rifles, RPGs, grenades and charges, and eliminated 17 terrorists. The Reconnaissance team had five wounded from a grenade thrown at them from a third floor. They captured the building and eliminated the terrorists.

I don't remember what else they said about the 7008th and 697th battalions. Our battalion continued investigating the layout of the tunnel found near the concrete factory. At the IDF level, I understood that the 143rd Division dealt with defense in the area. The 36th Division led a Golani attack on the fortress in Saja'iyya, very intense fighting followed. The 98th Division was operating in Khan Yunis, when an IED was activated on the division's remote commander center. The 99th Division was responsible for the corridor – and had no casualties. The 162th Division was responsible for clearing Beit Lahiya (20 terrorists eliminated and they have 40 terrorists captive). The 14th Brigade carried out stimulation operations for the sake of attacking the Shati refugee camp, and the 401st Brigade was managing the engagement with a significant tunnel found south of the Jabaliya Refugee Camp.

Immediately after the situational assessment, I went to sleep. I was so exhausted that I fell asleep with my helmet and vest on, even though it was a night I could have slept without the equipment. I slept so well that I didn't feel a thing.

Sunday, Fourth Night of Hanukkah, December 10, 2023

At 09:00 we held our morning briefing, and by 10:30, the team members who went to reinforce the deputy battalion commander's command center during the night returned to us. We had breakfast and continued doing what we've been doing here over the past days. At around 13:00, Suedi, Yemini, and I left for the deputy battalion commander's command center because it was important to me to verify various events that had occurred. We also wanted to see the "haul" that the battalion had found in the compound where we are currently stationed. Whenever we find weapons, charges, or intelligence, we pass it to Gidi, our battalion intelligence officer, and from there it goes to the complex in Bilu.

When we arrived, we found hundreds of Kalashnikov bullets, a pistol, dozens of magazines, vests, five Kalashnikovs, an RPG launcher, a PK machine gun, pistol holsters, magazines, and a lot of intelligence findings. On the lower floor, they kept all the charges and explosives we found. We're talking about tens of IEDs (EFPs, APLs, landmines, pipe bombs, and other improvised weapons), tens of hand grenades, mortar bombs, rocket launchers, and RPG warheads. In addition, there were all kinds of activation devices – electric tripwire and remote control devices. I made sure to document everything.

Around 15:30, Gevah came over the battalion radio and gave a speech in memory of Gal Eisenkot and Eyal Berkowitz. Suedi and Yemini wanted us to return to the team. Although I always like to be close to the battalion headquarters because it connects me to the bigger picture of the battle, we headed back to our stronghold.

On the way to the stronghold, we met Jake, who asked me if I had a detonating cord to bring him. My destructive instinct kicked in. "Why, what do you need to blow up?" I asked. There's no chance that something gets blown up around here without Yemini and I taking part in it. Turns out there's a huge transformer here that converts the electric voltage from high voltage to domestic voltage for the entire neighborhood, which is being used by Hamas for terrorist activity. It won't be here for long.

In short, after I made it clear to Jake that there's no way Yemini and I aren't participating in the blast, I ran up the stairs to our stronghold, pulled out all the explosives I had in my bag, and went downstairs. Suddenly, I heard a huge explosion from the school area in Korin's sector. I really hoped it wasn't an IED, and my fear was immediately proven wrong. The image of victory in this war stood in front of my eyes, or, more accurately, in front of the drone's camera.

About 250 men and terrorists were emerging one by one, handcuffed by both hands and feet, wearing underwear, and being led by IDF soldiers, with a look of fear and failure etched on their faces. There was not a drop of honor in them. A group of murderers, who until a few days ago celebrated the murder of our people, now walked meek and barefoot.

After I got to see the victory images from the drone's flight, I returned to my tasks: preparing the explosives for blowing up the transformer. Within five minutes we were breaking into the doors of the building where the device was located and got to work. Within a quarter of an hour, the entire place was beautifully rigged. The device was large, 3.5 by 2.5 meters, and located inside a machine room.

We moved back to stand at a safe distance from the blast, but not before I connected my Go-Pro to a nearby pillar. Unfortunately, we had to wait a long time for approval. We waited for around 40 minutes. But in the end we declared "ready to detonate," and we returned to our stronghold, tired but satisfied.

When I entered the building, there was an uncharacteristic silence. Usually, you can hear a radio in the background and the guys singing, but this time it was quiet. I shouted loudly, and there was no answer. I shouted again, this time louder. I was answered with "Kuno, be quiet." When I went upstairs, I saw that the team was having a conversation with the battalion commander. The team had already started to resent the fact that the senior level were not taking seriously the fact that we occasionally need to go home, to take care of our homes, businesses, and families. I don't know how much it helped, but it somewhat relieved the tension and nerves that the guys had in their stomachs. At the end of the conversation, we lit Hanukkah candles as a team and stayed to talk a bit.

After an hour of conversation, all the officers came for an officers' meeting at our stronghold. It was nice to see everyone. Kesten talked about a security mishap that happened to them, which by miracle did not end in six of our forces being killed. In short, it turns out that Rotem decided to rig one of the tunnels, claiming that we need to capture the terrorists before they attack us. I'm entirely with him up to this point. The problem was that we aren't trained for this and aren't aware of the issues that could happen as a result. The team lowered the explosives into the tunnel, but one of Kesten's team members wasn't sure if he had placed the charge correctly and decided to pull it back up to check it. All the while, Rotem was watching the camera monitor connected to the charge, hoping to spot a terrorist. Just as that soldier grabbed the charge and turned it to check that everything was set correctly, Rotem reported over the radio: "I identify hands! I Identify a face! A terrorist! A terrorist! Detonate the charge!"

Every time I recall this story, my heart starts beating fast. If not for Lahad and Agmon's cool-headedness, it would have ended differently. Since they were not sure that it was indeed a terrorist, they chose not to detonate the charge. Wow, a serious disaster was just averted. I heard that one of the soldiers who participated in this incident really went into trauma because of it. I was glad to hear that this event passed peacefully and ended up as nothing more than an investigation into a "near-miss."

Monday, Fifth Night of Hanukkah, December 11, 2023

In the morning I woke up for guard duty and went back to sleep until 08:00. Afterward, we got up, cleaned up the building. Then, I prayed, and took advantage of the free time, as always, for writing. Later I ate fried sausages for breakfast. It's amazing to see what the war brings out of me.

Later, we blew up the Feuer team's tunnel shafts, near the concrete factory, and the Snippe team's tunnel. After breakfast, we were informed that before we leave the Jabaliya zone, we need to destroy the entire area so that the terrorists have nothing to return to. Every building where we find weapons, ammunition, or signs of terror – we are to burn and blow up. "Half an hour to departure," Nahman declares. "Get your equipment ready for leaving."

Even though it's still morning, we are packing our "Turtles", the rear compartment of our vests, with supplies for 24 hours. We're supposed to return in the afternoon, but it has happened a few times that we plan for one thing and something else ends up happening. A few days ago, the teams from the 9th Company went out on an ambush, certain that it was only for a few hours, but the ambush ended up lasting more than a day. They returned starving, tired and exhausted. In short, we learned our lesson the hard way.

As soon as Nahman said we have half an hour until we leave, I decided to use the time for writing. Times of war are always the foundation of changes. I went upstairs and found a quiet writing nook near the snipers. From time to time I used them to verify details and events. I really like them, everyone there is so nice. After half an hour it was announced that there was a delay. It turns out that because of the explosion of the tunnels, all the buildings they intended to burn were destroyed. The tunnel layout passed right beneath the buildings, and the moment they were detonatcd the buildings simply collapsed.

It took about two more hours until we left. In the end, it was decided that we'd go to burn the House of Arches, a building that undoubtedly, in light of the findings we discovered, was used by Hamas. We went out in a company formation led by tanks, the Snippe team behind them with two tracker dogs, and us behind them with an engineering team.

We advanced and were pleased to see the destruction of the Hamas neighborhood, even though we felt that we needed to demolish it to its very foundations, to prevent terrorists from using it again. The moment we start getting closer we begin maneuvering, getting ourselves into the spirit. There's a concern about "Purple Rain," so we maintain greater distances. The Snippe team positions itself on a dirt embankment to provide cover fire and we prepare to maneuver towards the building. Malachi from the Snippe team opens fire with a Negev machine gun towards the building. Go Malachi! He gave a beautiful burst of fire. While they continue to provide covering fire, one of the Snippe team's soldiers "goes into matador mode" to open up a passage in the wall of the building. It works! There's an entry hole.

Nahman gives the order just before we start to storm the building and moves to jump up to the building entrance. The moment before we really get close to the building entrance and start to storm it, Nahman orders the dog handler to send a sniffer dog to scan for explosive material at the entrance, to rule out any IEDs. The dog handler sends the dog, and shortly after the dog sits at the building entrance. This happens a few times. Each time he sends her again to the building entrance the dog, just before entering the site, stops and sits down. When a sniffer dog sits near the building, it means it's rigged. What a miracle, I say to myself. If we hadn't sent the dog, there's a very high chance we would have entered and stepped on an explosive trap.

Nahman pulls back and while we take cover there, a tank fires two shells at the building. Thank God it ended like this and without casualties. We stay close to the scene for an hour, then pack up and head back to the bunker. It takes a lot of time to update all the sectors and forces in the area about movements, especially when the movements are outside the sector boundaries.

We returned to the detection post, offloaded our gear, and allowed ourselves to cool down a bit, since it was extremely hot during the mission. Again, I took the opportunity to write while the guys sat and talked. Kaneti, our excellent medic, suddenly calls out to me: "Kuno, come over here! Rotem wants to talk." As I come downstairs, the entire team is sitting in the living room while Rotem discusses the incident that occurred with Kesten's team. Over the last week, I really connected with the auxiliary team, and at least for now, I would have been happy to stay with them. The conversation doesn't really interest me. I sit quietly. Very uncharacteristic of me.

When Rotem asks what the guys have to say to him,

Suedi unloads at a thousand kilometers per hour. He says
– and rightly so – that we're tired of how the senior ranks
are treating us. Every time they promise a home visit,
they never follow through. It's clear to us all that we're in
a war, but we are already in our third month of fighting,
and since being drafted, we've barely been home, except
for four days after Beit Hanoun. All our other short
"refreshers" have been very short and unhelpful. They need
to understand that we've left behind families, businesses,
and many other responsibilities. We're very proud to fight
for our country and will be the first to stand up. At the end
of the day we are here, fighting at the most critical point.
But we're only asking for three days at home. I interject
and emphasize that if we knew it couldn't be arranged,
we would stay here without asking, but we see that it's
happening with other brigades, and it's only us who stay
behind.

After the conversation with Rotem, we continued talking
among ourselves. We unanimously decided that if we were
asked retrospectively whether we wanted to be in a combat
unit or not, the answer would be a definitive yes, without
exception, even if it required us to fight for a significantly
longer period. After finishing the talk with Rotem, we held
a team candle-lighting, and had a lavish dinner under the
direction of Chef Victor.

The night passed relatively quietly. Aside from the guard
shift at 21:00 which lasted an hour, I slept straight until
05:00, and at 06:00 I went back to sleep until 08:30.

Tuesday, Sixth Night of Hanukkah, December 12, 2023

Wow! This was the best night of sleep I've had during the war, and perhaps not just during the war, but ever. I slept amazingly! When I woke up, Kaneti came over and told me, "Kuno, you have the face of someone who slept well." We started the morning with a conversation with Nahman. The 7008th Battalion is going home today, and we are supposed to take over their positions and strongholds. We arrange our equipment.

Last night, I decided to take a shower. Since entering, I hadn't showered or changed clothes. We had a bathtub at our stronghold, so I cleaned it with water and bleach while I boiled a large pot of water on the gas. When the water boiled, I took the pot to the shower. Every time I filled half a bucket with cold water and another half with hot water and used the bucket like a showerhead. One of the most luxurious showers I've had. When I came out of the shower, I changed all my clothes. I think that's one of the reasons I slept so well, besides the fact that I didn't have a guard shift in the middle of the night.

We're arranging the equipment and getting ready to leave. The 10th Company is supposed to leave first, and we follow half an hour later. We use the time to have breakfast (pasta with sausages, salad, and garlic bread). Two days ago, Omer found gouache paints and brushes, so he's using the time to paint the walls. Honestly, he painted beautifully. Dotan, Amitai, and Suedi spent the time kicking a ball around. At 11:30, we were informed that we had another quarter-hour before leaving. We wanted to blow up the building, but it turns out the engineering team had already begun mining it. There's talk that they're going to blow up the entire Sheikh Zayed neighborhood. We start moving towards Tel Za'atar. On the way, we pass by the Indonesian hospital.

Overturned trucks were strewn all over the area of the hospital, apparently flipped and burnt in one of the bombings. I managed to see that one of the trucks had "Netzer Hazani" written on it and the other "Eli Sinai." Presumably, these were trucks that served the residents of Gush Katif before Israel's disengagement from Gaza. We start climbing towards Tel Za'atar, which, as its name suggests, is a mound. It overlooks the entire Jabaliya Refugee Camp, and we came here to allow bulldozers to continue working on the tunnels and to understand the layout of the tunnels passing through here.

After 25 minutes of walking, we reach our new stronghold, a three-story building. The problem in the camp is that everything is very compact, and there are narrow passages between the buildings, making it very difficult to prevent the arrival of terrorists. We're lucky that at the entrance to the stairs leading to the first and second floors, there is a gate that locks. We conduct a short briefing and start organizing the stronghold. While we did receive it from the Maglan team, it wasn't to a high standard. There are rumors that Duvdevan soldiers are less suited for combat and more for activities, making them inferior to other commando units. However, from what I've seen so far, while there certainly was a small gap at the beginning of the war, today there's no gap at all.

We quickly learned the small things that we were missing, a good example being the "fortified shelter." Initially, this entire subject was foreign to us. But if you were to enter our stronghold and compare it to a stronghold of the Maglan team, you would likely prefer ours.

We cleaned the apartment and sealed the house against the rain. Due to the bombings, most houses here have no windows and have cracks in the walls. We built a kitchen and gathered gas balloons and cooking utensils from other houses in the vicinity. We constructed bathrooms and even a shower. Later on, I'll describe in detail how. We hung blankets over the windows to ensure complete darkness. We brought blankets, mattresses, chairs, and cleaning supplies from nearby locations. We enhanced the observation posts and opened firing slits. After an hour and a half of intense teamwork, the house was ready. It's very satisfying. You get a house that looks bad and is barely inhabitable, and within an hour and a half, you turn it into a gem. Just before we finished the final touches, Nahman gathered us. What was so urgent that he had to stop us right before the end? Come on! Let us finish. That's the thought that crossed my mind at that moment. I stopped setting up the shower and went to sit down.

"Guys, listen up. I have something important to tell you. We found the bodies of two hostages. Thanks to us, they found their bodies." I felt a chills of emotion pass through me. This news was definitely worth stopping everything for! In the morning, just before we set out to replace 7008, I heard one of the team members say, "The country has set an impossible goal for itself." Indeed, bringing back all the hostages and missing persons sounded like something impossible, but after Nahman's message, I somehow was also filled with hope. I hoped we would find the hostages alive, not as bodies. But I also knew what it means to a family when they have someone to bury, and despite the great sorrow, I was proud that we attribute importance to the dead and make an effort to return them, even at the risk to our soldiers. I am glad to know that I have the right to participate in something so meaningful and historic. If only I knew how to explain in words how proud I am of this tremendous duty. Genuine pride, real pride, Jewish pride. When everything around us is burning and the smell of war hasn't subsided, our goal remains singular, refined, bright, unchanging. We are fighting an existential war which the State of Israel must win.

Nahman continued with his briefing, and once we finished, we returned to prepare the house. There is no greater joy than taking off the vest and shirt (and of course, for me, the tzitzit too), after sweating and working hard. Except for the four guys who remained on standby, we all took a moment to refresh. I seized the time to write. Victor in the kitchen is making us latkes from potatoes and beets he picked from one of the fields, in honor of Hanukkah. Just before the sun sets, Nahman halted for a moment and listened to the radio. "In a minute, they'll blow up the entire Sheikh Zayed neighborhood." The brigade commander said a few words over the radio. He spoke about our mission, about how we remember our fallen and counted backwards. 10… 9… 8… 3… 2… 1… a huge explosion!

Our entire building trembled. It was as if someone was holding the building and shaking it. For 2-3 minutes, I still felt the building continue to tremble. The cracks in the walls grew, and they were about 500-600 meters' aerial distance from the explosion. Within a few minutes, the skies were painted with ash and dust. The smell of smoke replaced the smell of winter. Heavy rain starts to fall. I tell myself, we need a lot of rain to wash away the evil that exists here. I'm not even sure there's enough rain in the world to clean this ground. Slowly, the ash and smoke from the explosion start to settle and flow into the streets. Streams of smoke and engine oil. The sky clears up, revealing a beautiful sunset in shades of red and pink. I wonder if Shiran is also watching the sunset now.

Night falls, and later the brigade's resupply arrives. A truck full of kit bags and heavy equipment. We quickly unload everything, standing in the middle of the street, dozens of soldiers and a massive truck. At any moment, we could be shot at. It's sheer chaos. We need to split the bags according to companies and teams, but it's pitch black. White light is out of the question, and given that the bags are marked in red spray paint, you can't see anything with red light. After 35 minutes, we finish without casualties. Later, I thought to myself that we need to install a lift on the trucks that would enable us to move the bags into a building with minimal soldiers outside. Anyway, we return to the stronghold, unpack our bags, and wait to see what we received this time. I must say, compared to last week, this week was a good haul. We finished arranging. Since we couldn't find Hanukkah candles, we improvised a menorah and lit it as a team. It turns out that we sang "Ma'oz Tzur" too loudly, because the battalion commander got on the radio irritated.

I was disappointed that I didn't have a letter from Shiran in the supply package. I really wanted one. Just before we went to sleep, Biton and two other team members came to our apartment with trays in hand. It turns out we have a delivery of sufganiyot (jelly-filled doughnuts). We told Omer that we really hope it's from the Roladin bakery because we're tired of military food. I want to give credit to the Shalit family. They own a Roladin branch in Netanya, and every time they hear they have a way to make soldiers happy, they are the first to contribute and help. I'm not just talking about during the war; even in normal times they are kind-hearted people.

I hear cheers coming from outside the stronghold, and I understand that it's the sufganiyot from the Shalit family – nothing else could explain the enthusiasm. Biton enters with 4 giant trays, 120 sufganiyot in various flavors – Oreo, pistachio, chocolate, dulce de leche... and lots of latkes. Now we can feel that it's Hanukkah! I went to sleep when I couldn't put another piece of sweetness into my mouth. The night shifts passed relatively quickly, and apart from the sounds of aircraft bombings, I didn't hear much.

Wednesday, 7th Night of Hanukkah, December 13, 2023

At 04:00, I woke up for guard duty. Meir said that one of the listeners from the 10th Company heard noises from the stairs below him, asked who it was, and received a burst from a Kalashnikov. It's a miracle no one was harmed. He promptly responded with a burst from a Negev, but didn't manage to hit the target. It turns out there was a tunnel close by, from which two terrorists came out of and tried to harm him. Apparently, those terrorists managed to escape back into the tunnel. That's how they fight, like mice. They know they have no chance against us, so they just try to hit and escape. At the end of the shift, I stayed to write and heard on the radio that there was a serious incident in Saja'iya. Many dead and injured. From what I understood, it was the commander of the Golani 13th Battalion, 2-3 company commanders, and 4-5 others dead. Curse the names of these mice.

When everyone woke up, Nahman left to plan a mission that would happen later that day, and we organized ourselves. It was a rainy morning. All the streets were flowing with water. There are all kinds of metrics for rain strength. Our metric was: how long does it take for you to go from dry to soaked. The measure stood at half a minute. Omer said, "It's a heavy rain." Nahman arrived and gave us a short briefing. The goal: to reach the site which controls the area and isolate it both from the south and the east, while the 9th Company captures southward and the engineers destroy 2 buildings that Hamas uses. After Nahman finished the briefing, Meir announced that Shaked would stay to guard this time, so I replaced him as a Negevist. We delayed our exit for an hour until the D9s arrived, so they could clear the route of IEDs while we moved to our destinations. Outside, there was heavy rain. The measurement stood between half a minute to a minute. We put on raincoats, which is always a dilemma: what do you prefer, to get soaking wet from rain or sweat? This time I chose sweat.

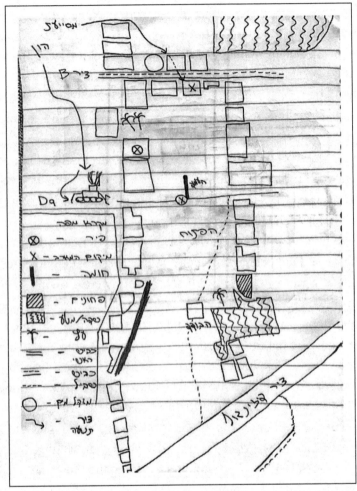

Ambush of Tel Za'atar[34]

---

34 This drawing depicts the progress and positioning of our forces. The dotted line in the middle is the path that the forces took in the open area, with buildings on either side. The circle with an x represents tunnel openings, and the long arrows represent the movement of the auxiliary and D9 forces.

We went outside and started walking. With each step, our shoes sank into the mud. Every shoe becomes a weight. Every step is a prayer, just not to fall and slip into the mud and puddles. The truth is that it's, more like a stream. This is how we advance up to the start point. The commanders go out to the observation post while the D9s open the southern axis. Nahman returns to us, and the Benny team starts capturing and clearing the building with the antenna. Hardly a wall is left standing after the Air Force bombings. After the Benny team finishes gaining control of the building, we go out to maneuver, and suddenly one of the D9s that opened the axis is hit by an anti-tank missile. The terrorist who came out of the nearby tunnel launched it and fled. One of the tanks spotted an observation cell to the east of us. We feel like we are in an active area.

We moved from the stronghold that the Benny team captured to our stronghold. We clear the ground floor and the first floor, identifying a locked door at −1. It's the heavy door of a shelter. Yemini and I breach the door using a prepared explosive charge and half a block of explosive material. It was an elegant explosion; I felt that we managed to accurately measure the amount of explosive material we needed. We gave the dust two minutes to settle and started searching. We found a large wood workshop but nothing beyond that. We finish scanning the building. We find some Hamas scarves and flags, a few pictures of martyrs, but nothing significant. After clearing the building, I assisted our snipers in setting up a post on the roof with a shooting slot and a southern facing observation point. There was an incredible view. The rain stopped, and suddenly, I realized how sweaty I was. I descended to the third floor where the rest of the team was. We had two guard posts, and the rest of the guys could rest. I brought out sausages, bread rolls, and ketchup and I ate. I finished half a can of tuna that I brought with me in my vest's turtle compartment. I gave the other half to Michaeli. Suddenly, Michaeli pulled out a giant bag of candy. It came at just the right time.

Jake, the auxiliary's company commander, and Nahman joined the gathering. Nahman mentioned that a few days before we replaced the 7008th Battalion in the zone, they found insane amounts of enemy documents and materials. They extracted safes full of intelligence from the site. I won't lie; I was a bit jealous.

I asked Michaeli for another handful of candy. Whoever invented gummies is a genius. It can truly be lifesaving sometimes.

While we sat and ate, Shlomi and Amitai spotted a terrorist walking on the Dizengoff axis and fired at him. They aimed at the stomach and pelvis, hitting the upper part of his right thigh. He managed to hop away on one leg until he disappeared, but unless a tourniquet was applied or pressure was placed within less than two minutes, it is highly likely he was killed. We stayed at this stronghold for a few hours. During this time, a few more people passed on the axis. Some of them were very old, so we didn't shoot at them, and some were in the relevant age group, but they moved quickly, so the snipers couldn't even release a shot. Apparently, I could have hit them with Negev bursts, but it wasn't operationally correct since it was an area threatened by RPG and anti-tank missiles, and we didn't want to expose our positions. Of course, if someone had identified us and opened fire, we would retaliate. And so the time passed. I was glad to hear that aside from some shards of glass from the D9's windshield, the operator wasn't seriously injured. Towards sunset, we began packing up. Just before we left, we threw a burst of fire. The firefight potentially exposed our position, but we did it because we knew we were abandoning it. We didn't know that a week later fighters from a parallel battalion would arrive at the location. I can't say for sure whether our firefight made the enemy more alert to this area, but I think that if we had known that we wouldn't be the last to operate there, we would have acted differently.

We returned to our stronghold drained, sweating, and with boots full of mud. It was time to use the shower I built. I placed two large pots of water on the gas and prepared the shower – a large plastic pail placed on a two-meter wooden structure I built. I made a hole in the pail, to the end of which I connected a hose with a tap, giving me control over the water's flow. Every time I want to shower, I boil a pot of water, pour it into the barrel, and add cold water until I reach the desired temperature. I showered for half an hour, rinsing off about 3-4 times. I used two six-packs of water, which is a lot! But since we were near the battalion's supply area, water wasn't a scarce commodity. When I finished, I dried off and changed into a clean uniform. I felt great. A shower is undoubtedly one of life's pleasures. I have a uniform that I wear during operations and combat, and another set that I wear during rest periods, only after I've showered. Later that evening, we lit Hanukkah candles.

An hour before the resupply arrived, I realized that Suedi was going back to Israel with the supply. I quickly wrote a letter to Shiran. Just as I brought it to Suedi, the supply truck arrived. We brought our bags with our equipment, unpacked them, and said goodbye to Suedi. This time, the bags were accompanied by letters, and, better yet – pictures came. I really enjoyed reading the letters, and the pictures were very moving. It's amazing that letters have come back into fashion. Shortly before we went to sleep, we were informed that they apparently found 4 more bodies in the tunnels.

There is something very important to understand. While we were fighting, we captured the Sheikh Zayed neighborhood and advanced towards capturing the Jabaliya Refugee Camp. We knew that there were several bodies of kidnapped and missing persons in the area. We received intelligence that Hamas is likely hiding the bodies in various areas, including tunnels, hoping that the IDF wouldn't find them. We grieved over every hostage that was killed, and it was very painful for us to know that there were numerous fatalities. The one comfort, which was in our hands, was the possibility of finding those bodies and bringing them back to Israel for a proper burial. The news of each found body was mixed with emotions. On one hand, there was joy in bringing them back to Israel and allowing families to mourn their loved ones and give them closure. But on the other hand, there was immense pain for yet another hostage who was killed and murdered by terrorists. I hoped that indeed these were the bodies of the kidnapped hostages that Hamas tried to hide from us.

Thursday, Eighth Night of Hanukkah, December 14, 2023

In the morning, after we woke up, Nahman went to the command post while we were getting organized and packing up. There was talk that we wouldn't be leaving for at least another 72 hours. It really upset the team, the understanding that we won't be out for Shabbat, and on top of that, the fact that we needed to pack up again and set up a new stronghold.

When Nahman returned, we understood that it was final. We need to leave the stronghold and return to the 9th Company. A few moments of grumbling, and then back to work. Nahman and 2-3 guys go out as a leading force to get a grasp of the upcoming missions and prepare the position we are about to get to. During this time, we pack up all our equipment and load all the food and other items we can't fit into our backpacks into crates. Even before I put on my gear, I realized it would be a nerve-wracking journey. Walking with heavy equipment in addition to walking through a threatened axis we haven't passed through yet, is a wonderful recipe for chaos. We went downstairs at around 12:00 ready for the move. Victor leads as Nahman has already advanced. We were a total of just ten soldiers, five of whom were fully equipped – i.e. didn't have the ability to return fire in case of issues. Just before the start of the movement, I identify Lahad leaving the deputy battalion commander's office. I asked him to lead the movement and suggested to Victor that Shlomi move back so there would be another gun close to us. It seemed to bother Shaked that I made the suggestion because at that moment, he exploded at me. I know it's a sensitive point. I often feel that I see the broader operational picture more precisely than the rest of the team. It probably stems from the fact that I myself was a team commander. But this is exactly where the problem lies. I came to the team as a soldier, and not as team commander, and I need to learn to take a step back. There are just moments where I feel that a slightly different approach could save lives. It's a kind of tension that I need to learn how to deal with. It was important to me that someone who actually knows the way leads the axis movement because we had advanced towards the place where the RPG incident on the D9 had happened just yesterday. I was glad that Lahad was with us.

We began moving. The ground was muddy, and the weights were heavy. Sometimes we let out a curse and continued. Lahad, the logistics officer, leads the team. At a certain point, we start moving through holes in the walls and courtyards of the strongholds, as the area is very exposed. It's a movement of about 100 meters that takes us around 20 minutes. There was a nervous atmosphere during the move, mainly among the guys at the back. At last we meet Nahman. He points out a site 20 meters west of us. We cross the 8th axis at a run and enter our three-story building. It feels like we are inside a refugee camp, although the building itself gives the sense of a house belonging to affluent people. We enter the building through a huge hole made in the wall and go up to the second floor. Within seconds, we start the "setting up a fortified home" mission, with each one playing their role. While the guys start setting up the stronghold, Nahman calls me to the balcony. He explains the force locations and threats in the area so that we can set up positions controlling the axes to our stronghold. By the way, he points and says, "Do you see the tree further down the street? There's the body of a terrorist there, a drone took him out this morning." I try to see what exactly he's talking about but I don't have a clear view of the body. The tree obscures it. It turns out we're located opposite the Nukhba operatives' strongholds, and apparently one of them was killed from the air this morning. When I looked back later using thermal technology, I identified a hot spot behind the tree. For a moment, I thought it was the terrorist's body, but I realized enough time had passed for the body to cool down, and it was likely an explosive. Either way, I understood that it was a place in which we needed to be sensitive and extra careful.

After an hour of work, Rotem and Lahad arrived to give us an introductory briefing. It had been a week and a half since we were with the 9th Company. It was a long discussion, about 40 minutes. I didn't have the energy. I was still irritated by Shaked's remark at the start of the movement, and I knew we had a lot more to do in setting up the stronghold. Rotem spoke about the necessity of our skills as Duvdevan soldiers in urban combat. At the end of the conversation, he took Nahman for a tour to familiarize him with the territory, while the rest of the teams in the company went out on a mission aimed at pushing the terrorists from east to west so that our positions and the 10th Company's positions would take them down. Betzel came on the radio to report that he identified terrorists and engaged them in fire. We continued arranging the house. First, I went up with Amitai and Shlomi to set up a sniper post on the 2nd floor. While I was breaking the wall to make a shooting hole, I accidentally struck my thumb with the hammer, cutting myself almost to the bone. I let out a scream. I quickly washed it with water and soap. Kaneti bandaged my finger while throwing out a remark like, "You're the biggest crybaby I've ever met." I wanted to respond to him that there's a reason some guys are constantly getting injured while others never seem to have anything happen to them, because they probably don't do much. But I stayed silent.

I went down with Amitai to enact the soundproofing protocol and to blackout the hole and the entrance to the building. It was a very large opening, and I feared that terrorists could come in through it without us noticing. In Saja'iya, there was an incident where we booby-trapped a house on the first floor, and the IEDs were set off without the soldiers knowing that the terrorists had actually entered the house. We sealed the house with lots of iron bars and metal we found. I was glad to see that we had a door with bolts, so we could lock the entrance.

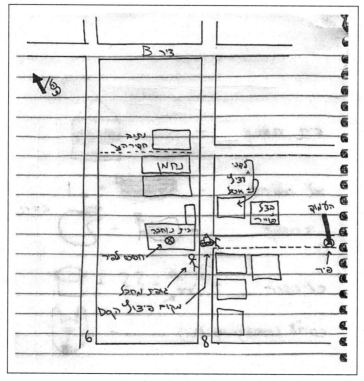

Jabaliya Refugee Camp[35]

While Amitai and I were arranging the entrance to the building, a tank from Rothman's unit arrived and asked him to cover them at close range. In hindsight, I should have told him that we couldn't, as it would create a situation where our positions would be too exposed. The sun was setting, and with it, fear began to rise. Suddenly, Nahman came on the radio to give a situational report. It turns out they had caught 150

35 This drawing depicts buildings, the location of IDF forces, the dead body of a terrorist, the location of the D9, several tunnel entrances (represented by circles with x's), penetration routes, and axes.

individuals, mostly women and children. He updates us that a convoy of around 50-60 terrorists will soon pass by, being taken for interrogation into Israel. It was a bizarre situation, and I couldn't quite understand what had happened there. I headed upstairs to update the team. Half of them were busy blacking out the windows with blankets or working on other tasks, and the other half were playing games. This irritated me in the moment, but Meir, as always, knows how to calm me down and make me see things positively.

I had rice and vegetables and sat down to talk with Shaked to set the record straight from the morning. It's amazing to see what a special team we have. We may argue and get frustrated, but in the end, we all appreciate and respect one another. In the morning, before we left the previous stronghold, the battalion rabbi had come to speak with us and shared an amazing and emotional letter his wife had written him. After reading the letter, he asked us a question. "Nahman team, what's your secret? You are the only team in the battalion or brigade in which no one, so far, has left the battle." We couldn't give him a single answer. It's Nahman, the banter, the commitment to the team, the ability to talk about difficulties too. One thing is certain – we have a powerful team.

When we left the stronghold, I brought with me eight candles and a menorah for the last candle lighting of Hanukkah. Now, after organizing the stronghold, I prepared the menorah for the lighting. Like with every eighth candle of Hanukkah, I wrote some wishes for the next year on a note. It seems I was overwhelmed with emotions at that moment, as a few friends laughed when they saw me tear up, and it really hurt me. I went to the side and told them to go ahead and light it without me. In many teams, the response might've been something along the lines of, "Let this crybaby have his moment," but not with us. They didn't give up on me and waited to light the candles together with me. Each member of our team has had tough moments, but ultimately, behind all the laughter, there is endless support. The tank came onto the radio identifying a lookout observing them. They quickly confirm with other soldiers, and the tank shoots at the lookout.

Just before I went on guard duty, the tank near us comes on the radio, reporting once again that it has identified a lookout. Within seconds, we confirm it's not our forces, and the tank fires towards the lookout, taking them down. During guard duty, I identify dozens of civilians walking southward and they are wearing sticklights. I understand that these are probably the civilians Nahman had spoken about over the radio, to let us know they were innocent and to protect their passage. When I finished my shift I did another personal candle lighting, and I placed the note under the menorah and went to sleep. I was exhausted from the day, but it didn't stop Shaked from waking me an hour later to open the building's door for Nahman who had come back from an outing with Rotem. He didn't know how to open the door, so I got up to open it. An hour passed after falling asleep again, and they woke me up for another guard shift. I was wiped out. I struggled to keep myself awake for the shift. It was a lying position, which made it hard for me to stay alert. During the shift I identified a movement in the vicinity and noticed a light in one of the nearby positions, but I didn't identify any more movement. I updated the guard to be aware and alert to this site, and finally, I went back to sleep.

Friday, December 15, 2023

We get up in the morning. Nahman is leading a briefing ahead of a mission. The goal: to push Hamas to the 8th axis and knock them out. We're moving within the refugee camp – ladders, narrow passages, rubble – and reach the first stronghold. The door is locked with a chain and lock. Dotan's precise shooting opens it. We enter, clear the area, and move on to the next site, a stronghold which, according to our intelligence, belongs to Nukhbah operatives. We enter the building, start scanning the building, and encounter a surprising sight: lots of parrots, some in cages, some just flying around inside the building. I felt sorry for them. I don't know exactly what post-traumatic parrots look like, but I think their appearance at that moment pretty much fit the definition. We break through the locked doors with explosives, and after a quick scan, we find piles of ammunition, weapons, mortar, a hand grenade, harnesses, and even IDF pants with a soldier's military ID. It later turned out that they belonged to a guy who was traveling abroad at the time, and his pants had been stolen years ago. After scanning the building, the battalion's engineering unit arrives to detonate it. They set mines on all the building's columns, and we withdrew from there.

During the detonation, the whole company sits in the

Atzitz team's building, and there's a lot of speculation about us leaving very soon. When we reach the stronghold, we are informed over the radio that we're packing up and heading home. Yes!!!! In a pack-up-to-go-home situation, the team always knows how to be the first prepared. The Feuer team secures the stronghold at the exit and we begin to leave. Oz fires smoke grenades on the 8th axis to facilitate a long maneuver across the axis. Michael prepares a smoke grenade but doesn't fire. When he got home, he discovered that he had a prepared smoke grenade in his gun. Luckily we have such rigorous safety protocols! We cross the axis in a difficult maneuver – a 150-meter leap with all the heavy gear on our backs. My pulse is through the roof! I haven't panted like this in a long time. We reach the Feuer team's stronghold, go up 4 floors, and position ourselves there until the 7008th Battalion replaces us. Yemini and I use the time to prepare charges for the next outing. The sun begins to set. A touching Shabbat prayer service. Home in just another moment. Kashi, Suedi, and I black-out the windows. Everyone gathers for Kiddush, and then we sit down to eat challah with the Atzitz team.

Some of the team members take the time to sleep, and some of us chat with the Feuer team. There's a good atmosphere. We do all sorts of impersonations of Vax the communicator and Rotem. Shlomi imitates Zanna, the auxiliary unit's sergeant. After talking with the guys from Feuer, I go to sleep. Kashi wakes me up after a while, "You need to get up! We're getting ready to leave." I organize the gear but, of course, we end up being delayed again. I go back to sleep.

At 00:30 the teams that are supposed to replace us arrive. We start moving. I didn't notice that the last step of the staircase was broken, and I fell down the stairs with all my equipment. Seems like I twisted my ankle. I felt a sharp pain in my left foot, but who cares when you're going home any minute. It seems that whoever was behind me didn't learn their lesson and also fell. We walked to the battalion's supply point. I limped a bit, but it's a short walk, and I distracted myself from the pain. A convoy of Humvees awaited us. During the ride towards the border, I talk with the soldier securing the convoy. He has avocado groves, which when combined with reserve duty is, let's just say, "challenging." We cross the border and reach the parking lot where buses are waiting for us. Just before boarding, the company sergeants shout, "Guys, come, we've got baguettes with schnitzel!" Turns out Shiran's parents and a few other parents prepared it for the whole company. I recognized immediately the baguettes Galia made. It's impossible not to. Such a nice gesture. From there, we head to the base at Bilu. We quickly unload all the gear to the logistics unit. Shiran waited for me outside the emergency supply unit. I was thrilled to see her, I was so excited to hug her. I know it's been a challenging period for her. Just before we leave, I meet Omer's Noa, say hello to her, and tell her how much I love Omer. Michael, a soldier in the company who also lives in Ra'anana, joins us for the ride. He had to go to the bathroom, but didn't want to go at the base. "Next time I use a bathroom, it's on a normal toilet and shower," he declared. I laughed, but I also understood him.

Finally, we made it home. How amazing! I open the

door and, to my surprise, I discover the air conditioning and lights have been on for two weeks straight since the last time we went back to reserve duty... Suddenly, it dawns on me and I shout, "Shit! The note!" "What note?" Shiran asks. "The note I placed under the menorah on the last night of Hanukkah," I explain. I had forgotten the menorah with the note where I wrote our requests for the upcoming year inside the stronghold in Jabaliya. Mine and Shiran's most private requests are now on a note inside an apartment in the heart of the Gaza Strip. Something about this piece of information rattles me. I imagine myself one day scrolling through my phone and unexpectedly stumbling upon a video of some Gazan explaining that the IDF's forces had been in his neighborhood, and as proof, he shows my menorah and burns the note in spite, or something of the kind. I hope that doesn't happen. I take a deep breath. The most important thing is that we returned home safely.

Finally, we had a normal Shabbat together. Wow, it's been too long. We took advantage of Sunday for some quality time together and in the evening we went out to a restaurant with Shiran's family. On Monday, my family dropped by for a visit. Some of them were still in the army, but I was glad to see those who came. We sat down for dinner, and right at the end of the meal, I received a message from my pre-army program's WhatsApp group: "With great sorrow, we write to inform you of the death of Etan Naeh, may he rest in peace, son of Avishai and Keren, may they be blessed, in battle in Gaza. Funeral details will be published shortly. We send love to the family and we share their deep sorrow."

Wait, what? This doesn't make sense. I read it again.

Etan Naeh fell in battle in southern Gaza. This hit me like a thunderclap. The last time I saw him, on October 7, I told him, "No silly business. No shenanigans or playing the hero," and he displayed that characteristic smile of his. I know they always say that the best ones go first, but Etan truly was the best. I told Shiran that Etan was the only person whose character traits I envied. I really remember the feeling of looking at someone and telling myself that I don't want his money, his appearance, or the respect people award him – I want his qualities. His humility, his diligence, his ability to look at every person around him and help them before they even ask. Etan was a source of admiration, the most modest person I've met in my life, and yet the most talented I've ever known.

The next day, we went to Etan's funeral at Sde Eliyahu. I couldn't believe we were saying goodbye to him. During the burial ceremony, while saying "El Male Rahamim," hundreds of birds suddenly appeared in the sky, dancing above Etan's grave. As soon as the ceremony ended, the birds flew away and disappeared as if they were never there. We felt that the entire universe was accompanying Etan on his final journey. I'm not usually one to believe in such things, but I couldn't remain indifferent. I was filled with respect for this wonderful person who left us just when we needed him most.

Rest in peace, dear friend. I know that wherever you go, you'll be the best at everything. I love you very much and I already miss you.

Fourth Notebook

Battle – Northern Gaza
5th Outing

Monday, December 25, 2023

My Shiran, the heroine! Last week we encountered a new difficulty we hadn't dealt with before. On one hand, the importance of taking part in the war effort is clear to both of us... but on the other hand, Shiran suffered from a lot of anxiety attacks. She was afraid something would happen to me. Unlike the rest of the team's partners, I can't lie to Shiran about what I've experienced, because she has access to the brigade's operational diary and controls every piece of information that concerns us. She sees the locations of our forces, and every event that occurs in our zone pops up on her screen.

On December 18, in the middle of my week-long vacation, we were informed of the killing of Daniel Ben Harosh, a former resident of Ra'anana whom I sometimes saw on Shabbat on the way to synagogue. Daniel, like me, served in the 551st Brigade, in a different battalion – the 6551st Battalion. Hearing about his fall was very painful, and we went to escort him on his final journey from his parents' home in Ra'anana to the cemetery. The next day, when we spoke, Shiran told me that the zone where Daniel fell was the zone our battalion was supposed to enter. This worried her to no end. I tried to calm her, but fear and anxiety are not rational things.

The morning after Daniel's death, we opened one of the

news sites and we saw the familiar face of Maoz Fenigstein, may his memory be blessed, a warrior from the Duvdevan unit who also fought in our brigade, in the 7008th Battalion. My heart sank. I met Maoz once or twice on base, and during that brief time, I had the privilege of meeting a special and joyful person. When I spoke with his team, I heard about a guy full of optimism and joy. A sensitive man who knew how to give comfort and support during hard times. A man with many dreams and aspirations who had a strong connection to our land and always wore a smile on his face. He fell in Jabaliya. Such pain. Shiran told me that Maoz studied in school with her in Canada when his family was on Shlihut[36] in Montreal. What a small world. Maoz's death also unsettled Shiran. Another fighter from my brigade had fallen. Another father and husband, who was supposed to return home safely, and who will not see his wife and his baby girl again.

It's clear to me that, on the one hand, my natural place is with the team, but Shiran had such a tough week that it's also clear that I can't leave her. I left the decision, about whether I should go back or not, up to her. I saw she was really suffering, torn between the fear of "losing me" and our shared desire to play a significant part in the war. This dilemma stayed with us throughout the week I was out. I felt her pain, but also felt that I had no way to ease it. It's a hard feeling. I knew one thing – that whatever decision Shiran would make, I would support her, no matter how hard it is. I promised myself that I would give her a sense of support,

---

36 A sabbatical year of service.

that I would be with her in her decision. At 9:00 on the last day she said, "Elkana, I'll take you back to base, but don't tell the team yet."

I saw and felt how much that sentence demanded from my Shiranush. She said it with a choked throat and great difficulty. Although she said it quietly and with a voice full of concern, a wave of pride flooded my body. I am amazed by the strength that Shiran has, and I know that for her to get those words out was more challenging than attacking terrorists. I always tell her, "Even though I'm the one fighting, all the credit belongs to you." The war of the military wives is incredibly tough, and she is handling it with supreme bravery. We prepared to leave – just this time we made sure the air conditioner and lights were off... The car was loaded up with a huge bag of coats and winter equipment that the Tzarfati family donated to us, two packets of cookies from "Night Cookie Ra'anana"... but the car was mostly full of worry.

We made a quick stop at Shiran's parents to say goodbye and left for Bilu. The journey went well. We discussed the great privilege we have. On the way, we had a conference call with my Uncle Roey, who serves at the Bilu base where he compiles all the operational information, and with my cousin Hillel, who serves in the armored corps and is supposed to enter Khan Younis. There's no doubt we can call ourselves a military family. Just counting our siblings and cousins, there are 15 of us currently serving. In the conversation, Roey reminded me that Shimeleh, Grandma Leah's brother, is also in the reserves at Bilu, and could help me with the bags at the checkpoint. I call Shimeleh and he immediately comes to help. I say a quick goodbye to Shiran so we don't delay him and then enter.

The time is 11:40, the entire battalion is in a conversation with the battalion commander and in the background there's the incredible smell of barbecue. I don't pay so much attention to the commander, and I'm generally being just happy about the decision to fight with the team. The battalion commander was spewing information about the various benefits for reservists, the number of terrorists we've eliminated in recent outings, the end of the fighting, and our readiness for the next outing. The team was hardly listening and was more busy hugging after a week of not seeing each other. After the battalion commander finished, we went to prepare the equipment for the next round. Food, explosives, ammunition, hygiene products, winter gear, and more... Even though the bags seemed to be ready, there's a lot to deal with. While organizing, I occasionally jumped up to grab steaks and chicken thighs from the barbecue.

It seems that some religious guy connected his phone to the sound system, because songs by Yaakov Shwekey and Yonatan Razel play non-stop in the background. At around 15:30, we begin to board the buses. I take the time to quickly write down a chapter of Psalms and another short prayer, which I promised Shiran during our drive to the base that I'd say every day. In previous outings, Shiran sent these as part of a letter, but this time I left all the letters at home because I didn't want them to get ruined. And since I don't remember them fully by heart, I wrote them down.

תפלה

" אול תירא נפתה פתאם ומשאת רשעים כי. תבא
הנ לבד ותפר. 3הדו זכה ולא יקום. כי. לנו אל
ול3 זקנה אני. הוא ולב שיבה אני. אסבל
אני עשית ואני. אנשא ואני. אסבל ואמלט: אך קריפם
131 לטשוך יטתו יסרית אך פניך :

" ענת כסמך לליש הגל כסב: יעלון: אשר נייהיה נאם
ונצופת אלהי. אגעלו גו. כי. הוא '3ילך עמם יקם
לבאר הדות . באהבתו ישך לך וקחא נפשו תחסה 3נה ושמה
אנתעו. לא תירא נפתך זילה אתל עלו ימום. לגהר באפל
יהלך נקמות יטוף בהרים. שמל על. שג3פך אלף ורבבה
נעינך אליך לא יגש. רק בעיך תביו. ושלמת רשעית ראה
כי. אתה י"היה נחסי. עליון שעת שעונך. לא תאונה אליך
רעה וגע לא יקרב באהלך. כי. מלאכיו יצוה לך
נשעך תכל ברכך. על כפים ישאונך פן תגף באל. באמן
רעלה על שחל ופתי תדרך תרמס כביר. ותין כי. בי. חשך ואפלטה
ואספ כתן כי. יגל שמי. ידשאנו ואדנהו לאו אנכי. נצבה אחלצם
לאבכבהו. ארך ינוים אלש ביזלהו ואר אהו ביטועתך."

תהילים פרק ג -

Psalms and Prayers[37]

---

37 Two prayers which I wrote in my diary so that I wouldn't forget to
say them each day that I was in Gaza.

The journey to the base of Zikim passed relatively quickly. Along the way, I wrote a few words to the pre-army preparation groups I lead. I feel that the unity that accompanied us since the start of the war is beginning to lose its strength, and it pains me deeply. When I was outside, in civilian life, I was exposed to a discourse that I hadn't heard since the sixth of October – all sorts of expressions which could take us back to that difficult and painful period. A divisive discourse. I make a point to steer clear of it; it's a discourse that doesn't exist between soldiers.

When we arrived at Zikim, we started feeling the atmosphere of war again. Lots of combat soldiers, each making final checks that their equipment is ready. We begin team briefings. Our mission this time is to secure a logistical route used by the 261st Division. As far as I understand, it's a less dangerous area than those we were in during our last outings, even though Daniel Ben Harosh, may his memory be blessed, was killed there a few days ago. The whole area is controlled by IDF forces, but it seems that there's a squad of terrorists in the area which manages to tail us. Nahman calls for us to board the Tatra trucks for departure. I call Shiran and talk to her just before we turn off our phones. They kept pushing me to hang up, but I wasn't interested. It was important for me to end the call smoothly.

When we get to the trucks, we find that they don't have seats or benches, just a low railing. "They say that all it takes is one bump and we'll be flying in the air," one of the guys says. We start climbing onto the cargo ramp and sit like sardines. The medical team of the company sits in the back and then it's us. Four rows of sardines, each of us with a large bag between our legs, whose only purpose right now is to make us lose the feeling in our legs. Everyone has exactly one second to decide how they want to sit because the moment the guy in front of you sits down, it becomes impossible to change position. The whole team gets on until the truck was filled with zero space left. Nahman announces, "Guys, everyone push back, there are still four more guys who need to get on". Through some miracle and a lot of effort, we all manage to get on. Of course, there's a delay, ten minutes that feel like forever. Nurit, Lahad's girlfriend who joined the platoon and takes care of everything we need, and Dekel, who is supposedly responsible for various HR matters but actually does much more, manage to take some pictures and we set off. At the border crossing, I say a prayer for safe travel and everyone responds loudly with "Amen". From there, we continue to a stronghold of the 162nd Division (their logistics unit), where we have an hour's wait until the transport team of the Reconnaissance battalion arrives and takes us to their zone. As usual, I went to one of the guys in the stronghold and asked him for treats and snacks for the guys. Five minutes later, I found myself with a large box full of snacks. I returned to the team and gave out the snacks and candy. While everyone is resting, I talk to our new doctor, who replaced Saar, our old doctor, and within a few minutes, the transport team arrives. We climb on the Humvees and after a relatively short drive, we arrive at our zone. We see that the guys we came to replace are very homesick. I really understand them. They were told that we would be replacing them at 11:00 this morning and it was already 1:30 at night. I don't know who told them that because it really wasn't logical that we would get there in that timeframe, but I understand why they were annoyed.

I asked one of the guys to "catch me up" on the zone, its threats, etc. He told me which strongholds are good and which less so. When we talked about threats, he told me, "Mainly baboons." What? "There's nothing here but baboons," he repeated. "The incidents happened on the front line." Again, I wasn't sure I understood what he meant; I assumed he was either teasing me or had a strange sense of humor. But then he explained that there's a zoo nearby which some of the animals had escaped from, including a group of about 4-5 baboons. There was also talk of a lioness, but he hadn't encountered her yet. "They move between the strongholds and eat some of our supplies," he added. Just before we parted, he gave me a bag full of gummy candies. I need to see those baboons!

All this time, the team commanders were touching base and handing down the orders for the new zone. It took quite a while, but eventually Nahman came back. Until he returned, Oz and I talked about the members of the unit who had fallen, hoping they would be the last. Amitai, who was sitting with us, suddenly said to me, "Kuno, do you know where Maoz fell?" I didn't know. "I think he fell in the sniper position you built, in an ambush we set up at Tel Za'atar near the Jabaliya refugee camp. I saw the picture of the position, and it looked exactly right. He was killed by enemy sniper fire."

This information was like a punch in the stomach. I was thrown into a tailspin. Could it be my fault? Perhaps I didn't build a secure enough position? Wait, what if it had happened when Shlomi and Amitai were at the post? What if it had happened while I was building the position? I realized I was asking myself too many "what if" questions and with some effort switched off those thoughts. It's hard to escape these questions, but they don't help anyone.[38]

Nahman asked two guys to join him for a sweep of the house we were supposed to enter. It was a captured area, and our stronghold had a team staying there until half an hour ago. Lahad, the logistics officer, gives us a site number, and we head towards it. We arrived at a blown-up and neglected stronghold, it was certainly not one that a team had just left. Nahman got on the radio and reported that we were likely given the wrong site number. It turns out we had scanned a site where no team had been – a site which could have had terrorists in it, and we were only three people. We returned to the point where the company was waiting for us, and this time we demanded that the new company commander of the zone lead us personally to the stronghold. Apparently, he just got confused with the location number he had given to Lahad earlier, because this time we entered a site adjacent to the one he had told us about. Another stupid mistake that could have cost lives. We scanned the site to understand how to set up the new defense position and called the team. The stronghold was relatively reasonable, but there was room for some more finishings. Within 40 minutes, we significantly

---

38 The number 217 is the unit's number which appears on many of its logos, and has become an "in-joke" among members of the Duvdevan unit.

elevated the stronghold. We sealed the windows and Nahman gave a briefing.

Entering Gaza for the fifth time doesn't feel the same anymore. It's no longer foreign to us. Recently, the fighting has become home and routine for me. Crossing the border no longer bothers me too much, and we are no longer afraid. That doesn't mean we are less cautious, on the contrary – I think we've learned to fight better. We simply got used to this crazy reality. A fine line separates a sense of security from irresponsible behavior, and I try to make sure I don't cross that line. We were exhausted and hungry, so I quickly prepared something to eat and went to sleep. The night guard shift passed quickly. I stood guard with Yemini, and we shared interesting conversations.

Tuesday, December 26, 2023

In the morning, when we woke up, Rotem's operations officer arrived at our stronghold. We organized things, and I made garlic bread for breakfast, but even before I managed to eat it, Nahman called all the squad commanders for a morning patrol of the zone, something that was supposed to take up to half an hour. The purpose of the patrol was to familiarize ourselves with the zone and locations of our forces. We set out, the Spear commanders (Shaked and Dotan), Squad commanders (Suedi and I), Victor (the sergeant), Nahman and Michaeli (comms), and we were joined by Biton and his radio operator.

We manage a relatively large zone in relation to the company, but we move quite quickly so that the patrol nears its end and I get closer to breakfast. When Rotem was with us, he said that the zone was relatively quiet and didn't have underground tunnels, so it was only a matter of time until Nahman found a tunnel. We continued on the patrol, and with a very shrewd detection of the "McNahman" (a combination of "machine" and "Nahman" – there's nothing else to say, the guy is a machine), we found a tunnel shaft hidden under a collapsed concrete beam from an adjacent building. This is the kind of thing that can be easily missed, but luckily Nahman is our commander. He's undoubtedly an asset. Michaeli tossed a grenade into the tunnel entrance and revealed another level. Another grenade from Suedi and we guard the entrance, ensuring no terrorist exits from it (this is what we call "freezing the tunnel") while Nahman updates the battalion. Our short patrol is prolonged. We stand in an adjacent building, and only then do we remember that we barely have water, food, or ammunition. After a brief deliberation, we turn back towards our stronghold while Dotan, Shaked, and Biton's radio operator stay behind to guard the tunnel entrance.

Very quickly, we "load up our turtles" with food, drink, ammunition, and night-vision goggles. When we returned, we each ate a little and took turns to guard the tunnel entrance. After a long discussion, it was decided that I would collapse the tunnel with explosives, and engineering tools would be brought tomorrow to examine it. I went with Michaeli and Rotem's radio operator to the auxiliary unit's stronghold to bring two more explosive mines and an additional nonel – a fifteen minute walk. It seems they have a nice stronghold. There, I met the auxiliary unit's Snippe and sniper teams, it was nice to see them. We gathered what we needed and returned to the tunnel. I attached the two mines, connected them with a detonation cord, and put them in a bag that will help me drop them into the pit. On the first attempt, there was a block obstructing the pit, so I removed the mines, threw a grenade, and then reinserted the mines. This time it worked. The mines went deep into the tunnel, we fixed them at the lower third of the tunnel and connected the nonel. We deployed it completely and connected it to the second nonel, so that all together we had a safe distance of about 100 meters. We made sure all forces were aware of the explosion and stood behind cover. A moment before detonation, Suedi gave an emotional speech over the radio in which he dedicated the explosion to the Nahman team and the refreshing break he just had, and all sorts of pearls of wisdom.

While Suedi counted backwards over the radio, I took the safety lock out of the ignition, and when he reached one – I detonated the pit. After the explosion, we returned to check its condition. It was completely destroyed, and the ground around it had caved in. Michaeli, who stood 2-3 meters from the pit, suddenly stumbled into it, and I quickly gave him a hand and warned the guys that the entire area was unstable, and to be careful. When I was standing near the tunnel entrance at noon I also suddenly fell inside, I'm not exactly sure why. Luckily I managed to stop myself from falling, otherwise, I would have found myself at the bottom. We decided to head back towards our stronghold, and when we arrived, a mouthwatering rice made by Victor was waiting for us. I was exhausted.

Sometimes war goes slowly, and sometimes it speeds up. When everything is running, you don't have time to think too much, and you are mainly focused on the here and now. But sometimes it stops, as if standing still. Outside, there are sounds of gunfire and explosions, but where you are, everything is quiet. It's a routine that demands your focus. In those moments, I am grateful that we have a radio. There is nothing more calming than music. The radio provides us with wonderful moments.

But there are also cursed moments, just like that evening. I listened to a song on the radio, and when the hour ended, the announcer came on and announced: "It has been released for publication that after fierce battles in the north of the Strip, during clashes with terrorists, two officers from the Nahal Brigade were killed. Major Shai Shamriz from Merkaz Shapira, a company commander in the 931st Battalion. Killed alongside him…" I stood up and stepped to the side. The announcer's voice was stable, but my heart trembled. I no longer cared who she would go on to say. Shai Shamriz? I checked with the team. Yes, it was undoubtedly him. I was lucky enough to meet Shai in training, and later he also served in Duvdevan. Like Etan Naeh, may he rest in peace, Shai was from my draft year. A special person, modest and quiet, to some extent it could be said that there were threads of similarities between him and Etan. He was a very special person.

I quickly calculated it. If I'm not mistaken, Shai is the 14th casualty from the Eli pre-army program since October

7th. At that moment, I hated the radio. I couldn't bear to hear it anymore. I felt how in the span of one moment, the pleasure of a beautiful song turned into grief with just three words, "Released for publication."

We were tired, and gradually the guys went to sleep. Nahman returned from the an officers' meeting, and tells us that a Maglan force entered a house in the south of the Strip, went in with grenades, and when they searched the room, they found a terrorist hiding under the bed. Thank God they didn't forget to use their grenades. We went to sleep, and I slept badly. Guard duty, the hour I "burned" while writing, and relentless thoughts about Shamriz didn't give me any rest.

Wednesday, December 27, 2023

In the morning, most of the company's teams went out for local missions, but we stayed at our stronghold and waited for the engineering team to come and investigate yesterday's tunnel. Meanwhile, a not-so-small drama happened. I went up to the top floor to use the bathroom and immediately after that, I went on guard duty. When I came down from guard duty, a few guys in the team pointed a finger of accusation towards me. It turns out that Kashi found a bag of shit on our mattress, and everyone said it was me. There were other suspects as well, but everyone denied it.

This might sound funny, but a real investigation was

opened. At first, Meir opened the bag to verify that it was indeed shit, and after his confirmation, the "investigators" wrote all the team members' names on the wall and interrogated each one individually. At one point, I was about to tell them that it was me, even though I had no connection to the story, just to put an end to the whole thing. However, a moment before I took the blame, I remembered that the Atzitz and Feuer teams' stronghold was next to us, so I said to Kashi, "Listen, there's a good chance it's someone from the Atzitz team who threw away his bag after they cleared up and left, and it flew into our stronghold through the window above your mattress."

After a moment of shock, everyone started laughing. We immediately went to the window, pushed aside the blanket we hung to darken the room, and our eyes were scarred! Above the window were 4-5 disgusting bags, with dozens more strewn near our building. It turned out that they had been throwing their bags in our direction since we arrived, and it was sheer luck that no one got hit so far.

The thorough investigation didn't end there; it simply shifted to the Atzitz team. I told Kashi that he owed me twice – first for falsely accusing me, and second because I didn't "confess," and therefore I prevented the possibility of a similar incident happening again (with the added option that this time the bag would tear, and its contents would spill over him while he slept…). We all laughed. We played chess and cards, and talked about the ping-pong tournament that will take place at the team gathering at Yemini's after the war.

It seems Nahman has already squeezed everything out of our stronghold, since he asked who wants to join him in scanning the adjacent stronghold. The idea was to set up a "fake defense," meaning a position that would look from the outside like it housed IDF forces, in order to deceive the enemy. Yemini, Shlomi, and I joined Nahman, and we set up a dummy stronghold at the adjacent building to ours. When we finished, we returned to our stronghold.

It turns out that there was a lot of chaos in the Gefen battalion's zone. In the morning, one of the Gefen forces went out to scan a site and found themselves encountering 6 terrorists face to face. Thankfully, the incident ended with two lightly wounded soldiers and all the terrorists killed. They informed us on the radio that the Gefen battalion's enlisted unit is scheduled to leave its zone to finish officer training, and we are supposed to replace them soon.

So, in a moment, our mission changed from discovering a tunnel and securing equipment – to replacing a team in a new zone and ambushing the enemy. From our experience in war, every time an IDF force disengages from a specific area, many terrorists come to see what we left behind in the strongholds, from food and drink to remnants of combat gear that were forgotten by mistake, all while collecting intelligence on our forces. The moment they approach to investigate the strongholds, they will fall straight into our ambush network. That's the plan at least.

At 15:30, we headed towards Gefen's zone, near

Darj Tufah. The journey was very bumpy, to the point that the door swung open after one of the bumps. When we arrived at the Gefen zone, we came to unload the armored personnel carrier and discovered a burnt and mutilated body underneath us. There was a terrible smell. Dogs approached the body and ate it. I felt nauseous. I don't know who that person was, but in their death they had not an ounce of dignity. It hurts me to see this; it's an unhealthy sight for the soul. The smell of the carcass was so strong that I felt like it stuck to my uniform. I don't know if it was psychological or if the smell really clung to me, but one thing is certain: the scent accompanied me for several hours. We arrived at the Gefen battalion commander's stronghold, where we waited for about half an hour before we began to move. Just before we left, I found a lot of explosive blocks and a roll of detonating cord, so I loaded everything into my bag. You never know when you might need explosives, and it's always better to have them on you in large quantities. Upon leaving the stronghold, we saw a platoon of Palhatz[39] or Paltatz[40] or something similar, but one thing is sure: they became the focus of attention. This was the first time we encountered female combatants in Gaza, and I saw how in an instant, like a group of baboons, our entire atmosphere changed. There was something funny about it. Gaza does its thing. Maybe it's not just Gaza.

We started walking. I probably overloaded, because my back screamed in pain: I went a bit overboard with the

---

39 Search and rescue unit.
40 Observation unit.

weight of my bag. The equipment I carried with me weighed around 75-80 kilograms.

After walking 150 meters, the Betzel team stops, and we follow them. We stand on the axis, in broad daylight, with a battle happening about 300 meters away from us, and we are completely exposed. Nahman is near the battalion commander's headquarters, because they asked him to wait and absorb the rest of the teams in the company, and I'm trying to understand what we are doing here and why we stopped.

After five minutes, we enter an adjacent site, and I crash onto my bag. In war, I discovered that there are two types of back pain related to bags: the pain felt while walking, and the pain the moment you take it off. I don't know which one of them is worse. Suedi takes out a packet of sunflower seeds, and I join him in eating them. Then the operations commander of the head of officer school entered. It turns out that the reason we didn't continue in the direction of the strongholds was because the guys from Gefen had burned down the strongholds that we were supposed to enter. Geniuses. Besides that, the fighting is taking them a lot longer than they expected.

Nahman came back to us, we reloaded our bags and started moving forward. Darkness fell, but I was too lazy to take out the night-vision goggles which were buried deep in my bag – definitely a poor decision. We walk on a steep slope, with heavy bags, on the ruins of a collapsed building, and with every step we take we run the risk of falling.

From the corner of my eye I notice a force approaching us and starting to mingle. I turn to one of the guys there and say to him, "Dude, don't you see that there's a team coming this way? Let us pass and go after us." A confused guy responds to me, "We're reservists, so we go first." For a moment, I thought he was joking, but he was being dead serious. I was a second away from slapping him in the face. It's not that they were older than us, if anything they were our age or younger; it's just because they have the cadets of the Gefen battalion with them, they act all high and mighty. Ridiculous. I have always hated the whole young-vs-veteran skirmiches, but encountering it in the midst of a war really got on my nerves. I calmed myself down quickly by realizing that they weren't worth my anger, and we continued walking. After another minute of progress, the force stopped by the roadside, and next to us, a convoy of several dozen surrendered terrorists passed us with their hands tied to their bodies, only wearing underwear. They are being led by soldiers, and I assume they are from the officer school unit.

I don't know what I think about it. On one hand, it's clear that I am happy to see these despicable terrorists walking defeated and desperate, led by IDF soldiers. But on the other hand, I can't come to terms with the fact that they are just going to spend a bit of time in an Israeli prison and likely be released in the next deal. Just a few minutes ago, they tried to kill my friends, and only when they realized that we were winning did they drop their weapons and raise their hands. One thing in this whole situation makes me happy. Recently, I see that the terrorists are starting to surrender en masse. Not one or two, but hundreds. Every area we reach, we witness that after a few days of fighting, lots of terrorists choose to surrender. The news that their fighting spirit is broken encourages me greatly.

The convoy of terrorists passes, and we continue to advance towards our new stronghold. In the background, sounds of war, soot, and flames from all directions. I hear that a Gefen soldier has been injured and they are evacuating him back to Israel. I shouted from a distance asking if they needed help, and they shouted back that they were managing. Conscripted soldiers, but heroes. Where is that stupid reservist?

We entered the stronghold that we were supposed to capture. While Squad C waited at the entrance, the Spear and Squad B went with Nahman to clear and capture it. Outside, it was all dark, except for the buildings burning around us. Nevertheless, we chose to scan the location with a flashlight to avoid traps. We understand that the site is less suitable for carrying out our ambush, and Squad B and the Spear set out to capture the adjacent location. In the meantime, we sit outside with our bags.

It barely took them a quarter of an hour to take over the new building, but for us, time passed slowly. We were worried about terrorists trying to approach us under the cover of the trees located to our east. This, combined with the fact that we have almost no night vision goggles, created an unpleasant pressure. Victor tried several times to make contact with Nahman over the radio, but to no avail. We wanted to advance to the building, but we didn't want to leave all the bags of the Spear team and Squad B behind. Finally, Nahman called us, and we began to move. We were already exhausted, but we knew that we had another long night ahead of us. We took comfort in knowing that we had finished walking with the bags for the next 48 hours, or at least until morning.

We had a small problem. Well, a small problem measuring 20 meters. Four tall trees stood in front of our target, blocking our field of vision to the east, and another palm tree blocked part of our line of vision southward. Yemini and I found ourselves rigging an explosive on the trees. We counted down, and in less than a second, we solved the problem. A eucalyptus tree of several tens of meters lays on the ground, and the whole top of the palm tree also caught fire and fell. After a successful first try, we prepared ourselves for the three remaining trees. While preparing the explosives for Operation "Eucalyptus Plowing 2," we received a message over the radio. For a moment, I thought I heard wrong, but very quickly, the smile and enthusiasm for the operation faded from our faces. The Gefen Battalion was loading ten buildings with charges, and for them to be able to detonate the buildings, we needed to go back to the battalion command headquarters. Exhausted and tired, we loaded our bags again and started moving back. I swear this was the toughest walk I've experienced in the war so far. We've had much longer walks, but this time the weight of the bag broke my back. I felt how, with every step I took, another vertebrae moved. Luckily, after twenty minutes of walking, it was finally over.

We were grumbling about the handling of the battalion and the brigade. We felt that something here wasn't planned right, and we couldn't quite understand why everything was so delayed. We were already waiting to hear the crazy explosion as we huddled on the floor in the warehouse beneath the battalion command headquarters. I reached into one of the compartments in my bag and pulled out the bag of candies that the soldier from the reconnaissance team gave me on the first day. It was amazing. Meir handed me a Coca Cola bottle he found, and in exchange, I offered him a large serving of gummies.

After half an hour, we heard the first explosion from a distance. An impressive explosion, but certainly not something that required us to go all the way back. While we were sitting in the warehouse, I hear that there are dozens, maybe even hundreds, of terrorists and civilians who surrendered and left the medical area and the surrounding sites. I go out together with Kaneti, Meir, Oz, and Victor to understand what's going on and if there's any way to help. When I stepped out, I was shocked. About 300 terrorists and civilians, all in the relevant age group, were sitting without clothes on, with their hands above their heads, some handcuffed and some not. We began to interrogate them.

We approached them with zip ties and called them out one by one while we handcuffed them – one of us handcuffed while the other covered for him. There's no doubt that the war is affecting me. In the beginning, it was hard for me to see people in such a state – humiliated, frightened, undignified – regardless of what they had done. Slowly, I got used to it. It's not healthy, even when it's the right thing to do. They deserve it, indeed, they deserve even worse. Every time I see the terrorists surrendering, I immediately think of the scenes from the communities surrounding Gaza on October 7th. When I think of October 7th, the intense hope to find the hostages alive is awakened within me again. I wanted to rescue the hostages so badly. The thought that maybe I'll be lucky enough to save them preoccupies me greatly. I shoot a quick glance back at the terrorists and return to reality. I hate doing this. Anyone who has turned themselves into a Hamas soldier deserves to die, but I would prefer not to harm my own soul. Like Oz said at the beginning of the war, "I would like to return as similar as possible to the person I was when I entered." We don't want to go through these difficult scenes, we just do what we must.

Suddenly, I saw one of the Gefen reservists enter the group of terrorists, instructing them to raise their hands and starting to handcuff them, while his gun, with a bullet in the chamber, freely swung from the strap around him. He was alone. "Are you stupid???" I shout at him in frustration. "How can you endanger all of us like this?! Just one plucky terrorist could grab the weapon and start shooting all around here!" I was already imagining how everything could turn into one huge bloodbath within moments.

I called the guy over and explained to him how dangerous it is, and in response, he said, "Shut up, you kid. Who are you to tell me how to handcuff?" I was stunned by his response. I didn't want to turn it into an incident right then and there, but undoubtedly, at the end of the war, this battalion needs to undergo an inspection. This is the second time that I've encountered this phenomenon among them within a few hours. Later, I understood that several guys on our team also experienced this more than once.

In any case, we continued handcuffing them while Meir, Michaeli, and Oz interrogated them, extracting crucial information about hostages, missing persons, Hamas operatives, and explosives in the area. After we finished, four Tatra trucks arrived to transport them for in-depth interrogation in Israel. The loading process for the Tatras took a long time. These are tall trucks, and we didn't have enough ladders. The fact that they were handcuffed and blindfolded didn't make the loading process any easier. They sat in five rows, each sitting with their legs spread so that the person in front could sit between their legs, just like we sat on these Tatras two and a half days ago.

It was already 2:00 AM, and they were shivering. One of the guys threw blankets over them. The situation was simply horrific; I have no other words for it. It's an inseparable part of the war, but I don't like it. When we finished, we returned to the team and went back to the battalion command headquarters until they updated us on the upcoming tasks. We sat there enjoying ourselves with the Kesten team. Moishe cracked jokes, and I tried to make use of the time by writing. After a while, the entire team went to sleep.

We heard a few more of Gefen's explosions. Not something that justified our returning all the way, but we had already come to terms with the situation. Not much time had passed and Nahman informed us that we're heading out to capture a new stronghold with the Atzitz team. The team tried to protest a bit, but to no use. During Nahman's briefing, they informed us that the resupply would arrive shortly at the battalion command headquarters. We decided to forgo the supplies. Our bags were already too heavy.

We set out in the direction of the new stronghold – a huge ten-storey building (including the roof), which ensures control over fire and observation of our zone. The building is located about 350 meters from the battalion commander headquarters, therefore the movement to it is not supposed to be particularly long. We arrive at the bus intersection and recognize the building. The Spear Squad goes up towards the Roladin axis, to identify if there is a comfortable entrance from there, but there isn't, so we enter through the eastern staircase. I don't know if you've ever captured a ten-storey building, but I can tell you it's a serious operation. At around the fifth floor we switch and the Atzitz team leads the operation. Here, too, we're speaking about a building of the wealthy – large, pretty and spacious, with an elevator that no longer worked. The apartments in the building were very large, around 250 meters per floor. Later we learned that apparently the building belongs to Haniyeh himself. Cheers to you, Haniyeh.

We decided to set up the stronghold quickly and to invest more in it tomorrow morning, after we rest. We sealed all the windows, we arranged mattresses, and we set up two guard positions. I made a hole in the wall so we could control the Roladin axis, and on the access route which leads out from the school and connects to Roladin. We're speaking about a hostile zone which is full of both civilians and terrorists. Through the hole, I discovered the body of a terrorist on the axis, eaten by dogs. It was a night with an almost full moon, so I didn't need to use night vision goggles. It was a disgusting sight, and I tried as much as I could not to look at it. We finished building the position and started tidying up the other rooms. One room was particularly smelly. It turns out that the homeowner had a Pomeranian dog that died under one of the beds. I didn't go to see it. I'd seen enough bodies for one day.

We closed the door, hoping that by tomorrow, when we come back, the dog won't be there. Nahman gave a night briefing, and the guys went to sleep. Despite my extreme tiredness, I used the time to write until my guard duty. Ten minutes before my shift, I was hit by terrible fatigue, and despite knowing it wasn't the best thing to do, I collapsed onto the mattress and dozed off until Kashi woke me up. The guard shift passed relatively quickly. We heard all sorts of sounds of metal dragging to the south of us, and a smoke trail rising from that area slightly affected our line of vision, but except for dogs (alive, thank goodness), I didn't see anyone crossing the axis. Finally, we went to sleep.

Thursday, December 28, 2023

At 06:30 I woke up to the sound of gunfire. Amitai and Shlomi identified a terrorist attempting to run across the axis. They shot at the center of the axis, but he managed to run back and disappear from their sight. Shlomi identified a definite hit in the upper abdomen. Later on, Nahman saw some terrorists evacuating him on a stretcher, but judging by the amount of blood he had lost, there was no chance he survived.

The whole area came alive this morning. Just as expected, many terrorists who were in the area began to attempt to understand where the forces had disappeared to since yesterday, and whether they had left any food supplies and intelligence materials. We understood that a large number of people would be involved, so we preferred to move up to the 8th floor where we would have better control over the axes.

Most of the guys continued sleeping, while six of us took positions upstairs. The goal: eliminate as many terrorists as possible. The method: allow the area to calm down, and as soon as the terrorists feel more comfortable moving between sites, fire accurate and comprehensive shots towards a large group of terrorists, while encircling with mortar and drone fire. We defined the red line in advance (the area from which shooting is carried out in order to kill) and the green line (the area from which enemy movement is reported).

Everything went according to plan. Slowly, the terrorists began moving freely on the axes, forgetting that we had just eliminated their "colleagues" in the zone. There was something challenging about it, as when you identify terrorists, you have the urge to neutralize them, but we didn't want to "burn" our positions. Suddenly, we spotted a group of 10-12 individuals sprinting across the axis from east to west. We almost opened fire on them, but at the last moment, we realized it was an IDF unit. It was the command center of the brigade. Idiots. Did they not think to inform us that they were entering our zone?

It turned out that one of the interrogations of the terrorists last night led to valuable intelligence findings in our zone. The brigade commander was eager to reach the location quickly, almost causing a friendly fire incident. They acted irresponsibly, moving uncoordinatedly and exposing themselves to significant risks. They quickly identified several strongholds with civilians hiding in them and began to investigate them. As soon as the incident became mass-scale, our operation command center, together with a number of interrogators from the company, went down and helped them in every stage of the investigation. When I looked out the window, I spotted another terrorist's body lying on the road about 150 meters away from us, and right next to the entrance which we had used to enter the building was a donkey carcass which seemed to have been injured by one of the explosions. It's strange that we didn't notice it last night.

Up until that moment, there was concern that Shlomi and Amitai hadn't "taken out" the terrorist from the morning, but that concern dissipated. From the southern window, a huge pool of blood was reflected. There's no chance anyone could survive losing so much blood. The pool was next to the stronghold where the civilians were hiding, and they are likely the ones who evacuated him on a stretcher. The interrogators separated the women and children from the men, and while they sent away the women and children so that they could search elsewhere, the men remained at the edge of the pavement without clothes, tied up with handcuffs. If you ask me, I don't know why women are always treated differently from the rest of the population. A woman can also pull out a weapon and shoot at you. History teaches us that there have been women who committed terrorist attacks, and more than just a handful, so why are we treating them differently here? God only knows. The situation is horrific generally speaking, but Hamas and other terror organizations are forcing us to deal with civilians with enormous levels of friction.

While the detainees waited for the truck to arrive to take them to Israel, Meir, Oz and Michaeli, who went down to interrogate the prisoners, discovered a number of important things. Meir received the names of five terrorists who took part in the events of the Black Shabbat, some of whom are likely still alive, along with other significant information. A moment before they started loading the prisoners onto the trucks, the owner of the apartment where the civilians were hiding called out to Meir. He told him that he had 2.5 million NIS (about 700,000 USD) in cash in the house, as well as an additional 130,000 USD which he had hidden. Meir didn't understand why he chose to tell him this. Perhaps he was trying to deceive us, and wanted to lead us to a trap. "If I leave the money in the house", said the man in Hebrew, "within a second, everyone here will steal it from me. But I trust you Israelis, you have honor. You won't steal it." Meir updated Rotem, and they entered the apartment.

It was a luxurious apartment that was built like a maze. Each room led to another. Meir didn't trust the owner and warned him in Arabic that nothing had better happen to them. After crossing the maze of rooms, they reached a locked room, where the homeowner opened the door and handed Meir two bags filled with money in cash and dollars. Meir asked him how they managed to survive in the apartment with so many people. The homeowner explained that he had dug a well to reach groundwater and they managed, at least in terms of drinking water.

I mostly used the rest of the day for writing, and occasionally stood guard. I had some good conversations with Shaked. I feel that during the war, we have become much closer. In one of the conversations with him, I told him about something terrible that has been affecting me every other day recently. When I eat meat or meat-like substances, the taste of meat in my mouth feels like the taste of flesh to me. At that moment, I am attacked by a terrible nausea that sometimes even makes me vomit, and from that moment I can't eat any more. I really hope this is temporary because it's a terrible feeling that I wouldn't wish on anyone.

The night fell, and we went to sleep early, very tired. During my second night shift, which was with Yemini, I saw a pack of dogs eating the body again; it was awful. I told Yemini about the food thing, and he told me off, "Kuno, stop with your nonsense! Just don't think about it; you'll give yourself PTSD." I somewhat agreed with what he said, but it's not always under my control.

It's crazy to see how the dogs started to act like a pack. I'd taken dogs for nice domesticated pets, unlike hyenas, foxes, and wolves. But apparently, the war has also affected the dogs. Packs of about ten dogs were roaming, looking for food and prey. You can always see clearly who leads the pack. It always impresses me to see how nature takes over everything in such a short time. I fell asleep quickly.

Friday, December 29, 2023

At 08:00 Nahman wakes us up and tells Meir and Michael to go at 08:40 to the Atzitz team because they need reinforcement in the interrogations. I asked to join. Oz and I stood up and quickly got ourselves ready to join them. Suddenly, I heard sniper shots, followed by a burst of gunfire. They spotted a terrorist. I don't know what he's made of, since even after the shooting he continued to move and crawl – he just didn't know that he was crawling in our direction. They shot at him again until he stopped moving. On one of the walls in the building was an X chart of terrorists that belonged to the previous team. Their count was at 12 X's, but our team had already surpassed their total.

Meir, Michaeli, Oz, and I went down to the Azitz team. We dubbed ourselves the "Hakshav Squad," POW investigators. We notified Atzitz that no matter what, we're going back to our stronghold at 12:00. We left the site, crossed the axis and the junction, and began to capture the outskirts of the Kasbah – a congested, complex, and dangerous area with narrow alleyways. We didn't find any civilians, and the time was already 11:20.

We managed to capture several houses and buildings and started to move deeper into the Kasbah. I felt relatively safe, but Oz and Meir said it was too much already. Meanwhile, Rotem updated over the radio that the Eshel team had to go secure the excavator, and the Azitz team needed to continue advancing to more sites. We notified them that we were leaving with the Eshel team, and we quickly disappeared with them to the "Mercedes" building, not far from the junction. When we arrived there, we saw all the battalion commanders and many soldiers. There was potential for another annoying task, so I told myself that we need to get the hell out of there at the first opportunity before the task catches us. The opportunity didn't take long to come. Two Humvees arrived at the location; they were supposed to return the battalion operation commander to the battalion command headquarters. Even before the battalion commander understood what was happening, I informed the drivers that we were traveling with them to our stronghold. By 11:37, we were already at our site. Tired but satisfied with the ride, we went up to the eighth floor of the building. Outside the building stood a Puma (Engineering Obstacle Breacher, an APC belonging to the engineering unit). When I entered the building, I noticed that mines were connected to all the building's pillars on the lower floors. It seems that one of the teams prepared the building for demolition. I didn't attach much importance to it and entered our stronghold. It took me about a quarter of an hour to dry off from all the sweat even after removing my uniform and vest.

We took advantage of the time to rest in the apartment, but the rest of the teams continued to fight, capture, and engage in "Shon" (hostages and missing persons searches). Like the past few days, terrorists surrendered today too. Nahman offered us, the "Hakshav Squad," to go down to help with all the captives. I, who was already wiped out from fatigue, decided to forgo the pleasure, but Meir and Oz went down. While they were interrogating the captives, I went on guard duty. I identified two women standing beside the soldiers. I asked what was going on, and they answered that one of them was going into labor and they were likely going to evacuate her to Israel. Indeed, later on, our off-road ambulance arrived to transfer her to a hospital in Israel.

A bit later, I asked about what happened with the guy from yesterday, and his 2.5 million shekels. They told me they had already interrogated him and realized he had no connection to Hamas, so they released him and sent him back along with all the money. The guy was actually telling the truth. Of course they will never mention our combat ethics! I don't think there is any other army that operates like that.

Suddenly, bursts of gunfire were heard from the Kasbah area, and I couldn't quite identify where from. I radioed the rest of the squads in our zone, but no one identified the source of the shooting. The company began to shoot towards suspicious locations. I scanned with binoculars to try and identify the source. One of the times I heard gunfire, I identified a burst of 3 Kalashnikov bullets from the southeast window of site 4300, an orange and brown multi-story building with an image of the Al-Aqsa Mosque on it. I went on the radio and reported the gunfire. Nahman, who was downstairs with Oz and Michaeli to guard the detainees, heard the report on the radio and understood it was a matter of seconds until I started firing towards the terrorist. He quickly ran through all the floors, and by the time he managed to arrive, I called Yemini to prepare the MAG for firing. Nahman panted like I hadn't seen him do in a long time. "I got you to do YALAM (fire after exertion), eh, Nahman?" I chuckled. Nahman smiled, "you have no idea!."

While we were updating the company about the origin of the gunfire, I sent Victor along with two other team members to replace Oz and Michaeli. They also sprinted for dear life, but unlike Nahman who went to deal with the radio, they immediately turned to engage the enemy.

It was simply insane. Yemini tore apart the building with MAG fire, but the real beauty began when Michaeli and Oz started firing with the grenade launcher. It seemed like they were born for this because on their very first shot, they managed to slip the grenade through the window of the terrorist's building from a distance of about 250 meters. And if that wasn't enough, two tank shell shots to the building sealed the deal. There wasn't much left of that terrorist. I finished guard duty. In the background, there were still sounds of war. Thick smoke billowed above dozens of buildings that were set ablaze. The sun started to set and we started preparing for Shabbat. It doesn't really mean much practically, but it was a kind of a conscious mood change for me.

I went down a few floors and saw Lahad talking on the phone. Nurit, his girlfriend, made sure we got a "kosher phone" approved for use. I immediately jumped on the opportunity and asked him for a chance to speak with Shiran. I tried to call, but there was no reception. While I could hear the Shabbat evening prayers from the Atzitz team's apartment, I hurried to the top floor to try to catch her again. After several failed attempts, I succeeded. I was so excited to hear her. I heard that she was really trying to hold back her tears, so I told Shiran that her pain is understandable and that she can freely share her difficulties with me. Shiran started to cry, and then stopped herself: "Elkana, know that it's hard for me, but I'm very proud of you." I missed my wife and her strength. Even when she is facing hardship, she manages to encourage and give me strength. We spoke for a quarter of an hour, and I enjoyed every moment. I'm so lucky to have such a special woman. We finished the conversation, and I went to pray with the Atzitz team. After the prayer, just before we returned to our stronghold, I suddenly remembered the mines I saw on the lower floors of the building. I told Lahad that we had to go down to unravel all the explosives. Many estimated I was going overboard, but I insisted. "Either we leave the building," I clarified, "or we disconnect everything." There was no chance we'd sleep inside a rigged building. A single anti-tank missile hit on the building would set off the mines, and instead of a localized incident with a few casualties, we would have nearly an entire company wiped out. Lahad was convinced and discussed it with Rotem. If I'm not mistaken, the Atzitz team spent a few hours afterwards packing up the mines. Sorry guys, it wasn't personal.

I entered our stronghold, where a Shabbat meal awaited us, full of great food made by Victor. Wow, it was incredible. There was soup and couscous, rice, spaghetti with sausages and onions, tahini, and a vegetable salad. High level.

When we sat down to eat, I noticed that I had lost my notebook, but before I started looking for it, I decided I would sit with the team for the Shabbat meal. A few attachments from the company also joined us, and they couldn't stop praising Victor. After we finished eating and talking, I went to look for the notebook. I wasn't afraid of losing it; I just worried someone might accidentally throw it in the garbage. After half an hour of searching, going up and down at least 200 steps, I found the notebook at Lahad's site. On my way up, I stopped at the Eshel team to check on them. It had been a long time since we talked. They asked me to read from the notebook, and they really flattered me. Besides complimenting the effort it takes to document, and my writing style, some of them jokingly asked, "Come on, Kuno, how much money do I need to pay to be included in the book?"

The Eshel team did an impressive job during the war. They started as a very young team, which you could feel at the beginning, but today they are without a doubt on a completely other level. An amazing crew. I went up and went to sleep. There was talk of a resupply soon, but I was already completely exhausted. I had one night shift.

Shabbat, December 30, 2023

I woke up early to make time for writing. At the beginning of the war, I spoke with one of my rabbis about keeping kosher during battle, and his response was clear: "Do what helps you be better fighters. Of course, where it is possible to observe and be stringent – it would be preferable, but if you feel the slightest doubt that it might benefit you as fighters, then there isn't even a question. The same goes for Shabbat and everything else." I felt that writing, even on Shabbat,[41] helped me as a soldier, without a shadow of a doubt. We are experiencing many significant and challenging events; writing helps me process these experiences and allows me to be a more composed combat soldier.

---

41 Writing is prohibited on Shabbat because it is considered a "creative" act, and Shabbat is meant to serve as a day of rest from "creative" acts.

I went down to Elad's floor, or "Ollar," and had the chance to talk with him. He is such a special person. Generally, I'm beginning to understand that our next mission as soldiers will be to rejoin civilian life and preserve the unity that was created between us, but this time – not just among the soldiers but among the entire nation. We must intensely love Israel. This is the only way we can succeed in avoiding disputes that would tear our society apart once again.

I go up to pray and say Kiddush. It's become a thing amongst our team to play chess. We spend every spare moment playing. After a sweet victory over Suedi and a bitter loss to Dotan, I went on guard duty. When I came down, Nahman announced that we would go out to scan for additional sites linked to Nukhba operatives, near the Kesten team's stronghold, hoping to find more weapons and maybe hostages.

A moment before we leave, we do a roll call at the entrance to the building. Suddenly, out of nowhere, or more correctly from the 10th floor, a blue bag was thrown out and made its way straight towards Michaeli. I could almost swear I saw it happen in slow motion. "Son of a bitch!!!" Michaeli roared, and those of us watching from the side didn't know whether to cry or to laugh. Michaeli's stress meter went from zero to one hundred in a second, but absolutely justifiably so. Just yesterday we were talking about how such a thing simply cannot be done in warfare. The bag was filled with shit. I write "was," because the moment it landed, it exploded over Michaeli's vest and weapon. Suddenly the phrase "they're throwing shit at me" took on a whole new meaning. It was a horrific situation! You just feel powerless. I've no idea what went through Michaeli's head in those seconds. Omer couldn't stop laughing.

Michaeli went up the stairs, cursing, until he reached the Eshel team's floor. He threw his vest at them and demanded they clean it. Victor and Suedi felt Michaeli's pain and followed him to help. I was speechless. The thought that it could have been me roused a wave of anxiety in me. How does something like this even happen? Don't they know not to throw bags towards the building's entrance?! He didn't even close the bag properly. Nahman snapped us out of our shock. "We have a mission to do," he said, not before ensuring that Michaeli was okay.

We moved towards the stronghold where the Feuer team was stationed. On our way, we passed by the body of a terrorist that smelled of decay, but that was nothing new for us. We started maneuvering. Something about this movement felt like a computer game. Everything feels so real yet, at the same time, like a scene from a war movie. All the while, I was thinking about Michaeli. "If it had happened to me, I would've lost it."

We move between holes we made in the walls and reach a burned and sooty building. The walls and concrete pillars are cracked from the heat and the fire. The ceramic tiles on the floor crumble under our shoes. Nahman comes over the radio and calls the Feuer team to come down and open the gate for us. We climbed two floors to the roof. There we met Biton and his operation commander, the sniper team, and part of the Feuer team. They immediately offered us gummies and candies, and we sat together in good spirits. The Feuer team was a bit grumpy because the brigade operation commander of the zone had set fire to a stronghold right next to them, and they could barely breathe.

We didn't stay there long. We went down from the building and maneuvered towards the first site we wanted to clear. Apart from Hamas flags, we didn't find much. After leaving the site, we burned it down and moved on to the next one, and so we passed a number of sites – each one was scanned, and as soon as we finished scanning, we set it on fire. The information on all these sites was obtained as a result of interrogations of terrorists in Israel, linking those buildings to Hamas.

It was 15:00 and we were already tired from the clearing, so we decided to pack up and return to the stronghold. I was preoccupied scanning the territory ahead, when suddenly I realized that my foot was about to land on the body of a terrorist in advanced stages of decay, but it was too late. I stepped straight on his face and felt parts of his facial bones break. A shiver ran through my entire body. I let out a barrage of heavy curses into the air and continued running. What an awful feeling! Certainly not something that makes the whole food and meat situation any easier. As we approached our building, we passed by a body lying near it. There was a sharp, awful stench of a carcass. I quickly passed it without looking.

At the entrance to the building, I wiped my shoes on the dirt for a good few minutes. I felt I had to distance myself from anything related to that body. In any case, I am a

Cohen;[42] I have never been near a cemetery and certainly not near dead bodies, and suddenly here I am experiencing this to the extreme. The climb back to our stronghold was long and tiring. I felt my muscles straining in every step. We were really worn out, and the heat didn't make it any easier on us. When we arrived, I immediately took off my vest, and the first thing I did was to vigorously wash and scrub my hands with soap.

Yesterday, I spoke with Shiran. She asked me, "Have you heard anything?" and when Shiran asks me in that tone, it means a friend of mine was killed. I replied to her, "Yes, such a pity about Shai Shamriz." "Yes…" she added. "And Shauli too." "Wait, what?" I got confused, "Which Shauli?" Shiran thought that if I had heard about Shai, I surely must have known about Shauli too. But I had no idea, and even now I couldn't understand who she was talking about. "Shauli Greenglick," she said, and I felt in one moment a huge lump begin to block my throat and fill my eyes with tears. "It can't be…" I whispered. Just a moment ago I heard his beautiful song on repeat. He truly was the most joyful person I knew, full of life. It doesn't make sense. "I'm sorry, Elkana. I was sure you had heard about him."

Shauli and Shai were killed in the same incident. It broke me. Every few hours, I found myself crying. We weren't the best of friends – we were each on the periphery of the other's social circle – but I loved and respected him, and in that moment, it was just too much. Too many friends and soldiers had been killed.

---

42 Jews descended from a priestly line, who are forbidden to come into close contact with anything considered religiously "impure," such as dead bodies.

I noticed how writing managed to bring me back to sanity, drawing out the anger and frustration that had built up inside me. Writing helps me organize my thoughts and helps me arrange all the experiences we are going through here. After an hour of writing, I felt that I had calmed down. I returned to the team, who were busy playing chess and Harry Potter trivia. Shabbat ended, we made Havdallah. Meir included blessings for the success of our people and soldiers in the ceremony: "May the nation of Israel succeed, may our soldiers succeed." There was something so natural and genuine in these blessings. A simple desire to be healthy and whole, to return to our families, to know that all the hostages would return to their families safely.

Nahman gave us a night briefing in our improvised living room. Some of us sitting, some standing. In the corner of the room, a few friends tried to call home with the new cell phone that Nurit had managed to get us. She's a real trooper. It was hard for her not to be able to communicate with Lahad during the war, so she decided to join our company and drafted to the reserves. Nurit was responsible for all logistical matters and fundraising for the combat soldiers. A fearless woman. If it were up to her, we would probably even see her in Gaza. Kashi, who was standing near one of the walls, began to draw "Hangman" on the wall. Gradually, we were all drawn into his riddles. Nahman joined in and added his own. We started with classic riddles, like "Which seven countries in the world have names which don't contain the letters A, E, I, O, or U?" We moved on to more difficult puzzles and to drawing riddles on the wall. All of them were related to the war.

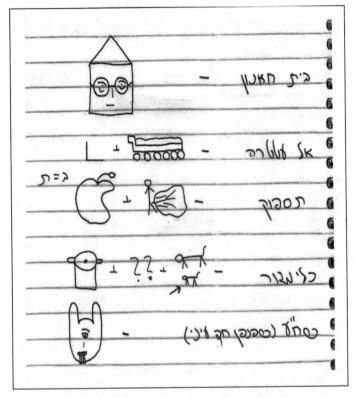

Drawings of the riddles[43]

Nahman went out for a briefing with the team commanders in preparation for tomorrow, and we began getting ready for bed. There's already a lot of talk in the

43 Some examples of riddles, which are meant to be read from left to right. The picture is the riddle, and the words to the right of them are the answer. For example, the answer to the first clue is "Beit Hanoun", which is a neighborhood in Gaza. The word "Beit" means house, and the word "Hanoun" sounds similar to the Hebrew word "Henun", which means "nerd". Hence, a nerdy house.

air about the entire brigade leaving Gaza soon, but I try as much as possible not to think about it. Right now, we're here, and that's what should occupy us. When Nahman returns, he informs us that early tomorrow morning we're going to replace the 14th Brigade. They are located to the north of Shati, not far from where we were at the start of the current round, though a bit closer to Gaza City.

The plan was to leave by foot towards the battalion commander's house and from there to continue on Tatra trucks to our destination. We didn't know exactly where we were supposed to be dropped off, and we understood that the drop-off point would only be decided tomorrow. We packed up and closed our bags and got ready to sleep.

I managed to talk to Shiran on the phone for a moment. Shiran asked me when we were supposed to leave, so I told her that in war everything can change at any moment, but probably in the upcoming days. I wanted to talk to her a bit more, but the call was disconnected. Suedi was waiting for his turn on the phone, so I didn't want to steal his precious time. At least I managed to hear her a little. I went to sleep. The night shift passed relatively quickly.

Sunday, December 31, 2023

At 03:45 we wake up and get ready to leave. During the night, we managed to return all the sealed food supplies that were left over, as we knew we wouldn't be able to drag them with us. We loaded everything onto a convoy of Humvees that arrived. Nahman gave a briefing ahead of our move to the new zone.

The IDF is slowly trying to withdraw the reserve forces from Gaza and use the enlisted forces more broadly. The goal: to establish a security axis that would allow control over Gaza through outposts from which IDF forces would conduct missions. Generally, from what I understand, the war is divided into four phases:

A. A powerful fire campaign – what we saw at the beginning of the war. A lot of shelling and artillery fire.

B. Gradual and evolving maneuvers in the northern Strip, Khan Younis, and central camps – i.e., everything we have done so far in ground maneuvering.

C. Deepening of the gains and completion of the dismantlement of Hamas – denying Hamas any capability (for up to a year).

D. "The day after" – civilian stabilization and restructuring of all the arenas of the war.

We understand that the army is starting to move towards stage C of the battle. At this very moment, IDF soldiers are fighting the last strongholds held by Hamas in the Strip. My battalion is replacing the battalion from the 14th Brigade, and on Monday, the Nahal soldiers will replace us. The goal: to defend the Dekel axis and to control, by fire and surveillance, the northern parts of the Shati refugee camp and Rimal neighborhood, in order to allow the division to build a line of outposts for the next stage of the fighting. Of course, while we're there, we are expected to continue scanning and clearing the area of enemies and combat capabilities.

Nahman finishes the briefing, and we start getting our gear on and packing up. Just before the company leaves the building, we make sure to rig it with 20 mines placed on the building's pillars. The fact that the building likely belongs to Ismail Haniyeh makes the explosion much more significant for me. Victor runs through the roll call, and we start moving towards the battalion commander's house. Outside, everything is quiet and dark. Except for the occasional bark which can be heard, it seems like everyone is still asleep. A cool breeze blows from the west, reminding me that we are still at war. For a moment, I debated putting on night-vision goggles, but they give me a very tunnel-like vision, and it happened to be a moonlit night, allowing us to see quite well. When walking through ruins, it's better to avoid using night-vision goggles.

We arrive at the battalion commander's house, where we discover that the 14th Brigade's exit is delayed. I'm not surprised. During the war so far, I haven't once found myself in a situation where everything goes according to plan, and there's no reason it should suddenly happen now. Everyone puts their bags down, spreads out their mattresses, and gets ready for sleep. I decided to make use of the time for writing. The table at the stronghold was messy, dirty, and damp, so I took a shirt I found in one of the closets and used it to clean the table a bit. We're accustomed to living with constraints here, and we're naturally resourceful so we can make limited equipment go a long way. I created a dry and clean "island" for myself and started writing.

When I finished, I left the room and saw the company's doctor, Amir Ben Yehuda. "How convenient, you're exactly who I need," I said to him. Last Tuesday, when we went on a tour in the zone with Nahman, we found a tunnel entrance. When I approached the tunnel to take a photo of it, I tripped and stumbled – not really into it, but enough to receive a strong hit to my knee and palm of my hand. I didn't pay it much attention, but when I woke up the next morning, I discovered that my whole body was aching from the fall and that the hand injury didn't look good. Over the past week, I tried to ignore the pain, and it did indeed slowly disappear. Every day, I made sure to wash the hand and disinfect it with alcohol, but apparently, it wasn't enough. The dirt and diseases in our environment were not good for a wound. I noticed that with every day that passed, the wound continued to fester. It was covered with a yellow pus, and a redness formed around it, causing me pain with every movement. The doctor immediately understood what had happened and promptly fetched his bag to bring me an ointment to fight infection.

I'm not just writing about this for the sake of it. One of the most annoying things in combat is when you're asked to fetch something from deep inside a bag. I expected the doctor to say something like "come back in an hour," and I promise I would've understood him. But not our doctor! He immediately opened his bag and emptied its contents until he got to the ointment. People are judged by all sorts of moments in their lives, and at that moment, I highly appreciated him.

Amir, the medic, made sure to disinfect the wound and apply the ointment. We have an excellent medical team in our company! In my opinion, medical teams are tested in moments of routine. If they excel even when things are boring and dull, it's a sign that they'll also excel in emergencies and extreme events.

There is a strong metric that helps in assessing workplaces and study institutions – go straight to their restrooms. If they are clean and tidy, it's likely a good and serious institution. If they are dirty, I would recommend staying away from the institution.

In any case, I found myself a room to sleep in. I had barely laid down on the mattress when I suddenly heard noises outside very close to our building. I quickly approached the window, pulled aside the blackout curtain, and to my surprise, I discovered a horse walking amongst the rubble and eating from the piles of trash and food that had accumulated around the battalion commander's house. I returned to my mattress, and before I could even close my eyes, I drifted off to sleep.

At 10:00, Suedi called me for guard duty. We had two positions in the entire building – a listening post on the staircase and another position with the Kesten team. It's not technically ideal, as we need to have control over everything happening around the building, but since we were in the frame of mind of "we're leaving the building at any moment and climbing onto the Tatra trucks," we didn't set up the positions.

By 11:00, most of the team was awake, but there wasn't much to do yet. Mostly, we waited to be told to climb onto the Tatras. Suddenly, we heard Arabic chatter from the northern window. To be honest, I was busy writing and didn't pay much attention until Yemini exclaimed, "I think there are

Arabs under the building" – the same window where just a few hours ago, I had seen the horse.

As if I had forgotten that we were in a war, I rushed to open the window, without a vest, without a helmet, and without a weapon. I stuck my head out the window and counted about ten men, all fighting age, collecting food from the same heap the horse had eaten from. They didn't notice me. Anyone looking at them from the side would pity them, but it was clear that men of this age still roaming the area were undoubtedly terrorists. We couldn't let anyone come too close to us; it could end in a terrible disaster. They could rig the entrance to the building, or worse, collapse the building while we were still inside. I don't know how it happened without us noticing, but we needed to get them away.

Yemini ran to get a weapon, and Oz, who was lying on the mattress, jumped to his feet and ran towards the window. "Wow, whoa, wow," Oz shouted towards the group of men, who continued to be engrossed in the food and trash heap. Perhaps they had thought we had left the area. Oz fired in their direction and shouted "warning shots." I wasn't wearing ear plugs and felt every shot from Oz damage my hearing.

As in slow motion, we saw the group of men beginning to disperse. Yemini also approached the window and started firing in their direction. Every shot that hit the ground sent sand particles flying. The fire caught the trash heap and began to burn everything around it. My ears were hot and painful. I heard a loud ringing in my right ear and felt a sharp pain. Looking at the floor of the room, I realized I had been standing on Suedi the whole time, who was lying on the mattress. I pulled out earplugs from my shirt pocket and put them in my ears, as if they would help.

Immediately after the event, we tried to investigate what had happened. We understood that Oz hadn't noticed himself shouting at them before starting to shoot towards them. We also understood the significance of orders and semantics. The description of a situation can influence the way we choose to act: it is likely that if Oz had shouted "terrorist!" the entire situation would have looked completely different.

As we speak, thick smoke began to fill the building. Nahman and Dotan went down to try to put out the fire. The firefighting team arrived with blankets and attempted to smother it. The Kesten team poured water from the upper floors. In the end, they succeeded, and the fire was extinguished. Later, an excavator arrived to clear the trash, and made sure to put out the embers that remained.

We continued to wait. The guys played chess, cooked, and passed the time. I was on guard duty, I heard a request over the radio for the rabbinical scanning unit[44] to come with masks and bags for at least ten bodies. I didn't quite understand what they were doing, but I assumed they were collecting a large quantity of body parts. I hoped that we could at least return more brothers to be buried properly in Israel.

I can't explain this transition, from dealing with hostages to playing chess. It's not indifference, it's more about being mission-driven. The mind is always focused on what is in

---

44 The team charged with collecting every last drop of blood and body part, to ensure that fallen soldiers and hostages receive a dignified burial according to Jewish law.

front of it now. If there's a terrorist, we shoot. If there are hostages found, we deal with them. If there's chess, we play. That's the only way to maintain sanity in war.

The sun began to set. I played chess against Lahad, but he beat me. I thought to myself that it was a shame that Dvir, my brother, isn't here with me; I'm sure he would have won. Every time Dvir plays, I'm proud of him. In general, we're a very loving family where everyone is proud of each other. There's no doubt I'm lucky to have such an amazing family. Wow, I miss them.

Nahman announced that we are preparing to pack up soon. I hoped we would blow up the battalion HQ like we did in the morning when we blew up the previous building we were in, but it was decided that we would burn it down. I took the mission upon myself. I went with Yemini up to the 7th floor and began to prepare the building for the fire. Luckily, almost every apartment held a 24-liter jerry can full of olive oil in the kitchen, which made the task much easier. In each apartment, I made sure to connect all the furniture made of wood and fabric, poured oil on the mattresses, and ensured that the most flammable parts were connected. All that was left was to ignite the fire and open the windows to allow air into the apartment to feed the fire.

Victor yelled for us to come down. The Eshel team received the honor of setting the building on fire. I was a bit disappointed because after all our efforts, I wanted to be the one to set it ablaze, but I consoled myself with the fact that at least I wouldn't smell of smoke and soot. And on second thought, it didn't really matter, because we're all dirty and smelly as we are... I put on my gear and went down. When

I lifted the bag, I remembered how much I hadn't missed the weight of the equipment. I left the building and headed towards the trucks waiting for us outside. I was satisfied. Tatras with experienced drivers of the 551st Brigade – we were sorted. However, it turns out that everyone else was boarding the Tatras, and our team was getting on the "Rio," which is like a Tatra but smaller and more cramped. We board, squashed like crazy, and we wait. One of the guys behind me thinks it's time to give me a rap on the helmet. Without the ability to react or look back, I shout, "The next person who does this, I'll break his face."

"Why the hell aren't we leaving?" Kaneti gets irritated. We understood that the whole company was waiting for the Eshel team to burn the building. "What's taking them so long?" I think to myself, after all, we already did all the work for them. Thick smoke begins to emerge from the upper floors, but flames are barely visible. Slowly, very slowly, the fire begins to spread in the southern wing of the building. Yemini and I start getting annoyed because if we had done the job, the building would already be engulfed in flames. Yemini immediately adds, "These idiots didn't open the windows." We've already burned down one or two buildings in Gaza, and we know at what speed the entire structure goes up in flames. Another hit to the helmet! I try to turn around and understand who it was, but I can't move. Everyone is quiet, no one reacts. Time passes, and we start losing sensation in our legs. Someone yells from behind, "We'd be better off just walking," but I remind myself how awful it is to walk with these weights. The Eshel team boards the Tatras and reports through the radio, "The building is burning." Yeah, sure. There's barely anything there on fire! At long last, we start moving. While I still have a visual connection with the building, I hope to see flames from one of the windows and check that the building burns along with the equipment, messages, and lists of frequencies on the walls. A moment before we turn and disappear, I spot a few small flames emerging from one of the windows on the upper floors. I hope that is enough.

As we progress in our journey, I realize that the Tatras are not the only thing I was wrong about. The drivers are probably not 551 either. At every stop and brake, a red light ignites on the back of the truck. It's supposed to be a journey in total darkness. We are driving through the middle of Gaza! Every light could expose us and lead to a serious altercation! I recited the prayer for safe travel like I had never done in my life and said to Nahman, "Tell those idiots over the radio to turn off the lights." It didn't help. The journey was horrific, I have no other word for it. The driver barely managed to shift gears without the truck trembling. Suddenly, I realized the truck had stopped in place, and of course, any terrorist within a kilometer and a half range could identify it because of the rear lights that were on.

Just don't hit us with a missile, I pray, while I run through dozens of scenarios in my head. Why on earth were we stopping, and with this red light on? It turns out the driver got confused with navigation. Over twenty soldiers were sitting on a truck in the middle of Gaza, marked by the rear lights of our truck, unable to move because of the heavy bags piled on them. I was getting anxious. And as if all of that wasn't enough, I get another knock on my helmet.

Someone on the team really wanted to test my limits. I've noticed that in situations like these, I don't always behave correctly, and could easily cloud the atmosphere and stress the team out. So, I told myself to calm down and hope that everything will be fine, while I suggested to Nahman to use the company radio to ask one of our navigators to go up to the driver's cabin and guide them. We turn, and after five minutes of driving, we reach the junction we missed. The road is bumpy, and at any moment, I feel like I'm falling off the truck. My right hand is holding onto Yemini's foot, and my left hand is gripping the truck's railing with all my strength. Behind me, Kaneti is suffering under the pressure that my ceramic vest is exerting on his foot, while my legs have completely lost sensation. I decided to calm down, breathe deeply, and simply wait for it to pass. Stress and nerves never do any good. Without warning, I feel a sharp pain in my left hand as I let out a fierce curse. If no one has identified us so far, my scream probably exposed the entire force. This idiot driver was driving right next to the rubble of a building during the journey, and a nail sticking out from the rubble grazed my palm. It was a miracle it didn't pierce my hand. I could actually end up surviving two months of fighting in Gaza and lose a hand because of a truck ride.

When we arrived, I got off and approached the driver. "Dude, tell me, have you ever driven a truck in the dark? Have you ever driven with night goggles on?" And he answered, "Honestly, no."

At this point, I lost it.

"Listen," I told him. "I don't know what you're doing here. Maybe you came here because you wanted to put

Gaza on your resume, but one thing is certain – you are irresponsible. This was the worst journey I've ever been on in Gaza. Do you realize you have 25 soldiers on the truck, and any mistake of yours could lead to our deaths? How does it make any sense that you are driving with your rear lights on? And how do you lose sight of the convoy in the middle of a hostile area while driving? Do you know you almost chopped off my hand when you drove into the rubble there?"

His commander approached me and said, "Alright, calm down, he just came to do good."

"I don't need your favors. You guys could have killed us." I stood up and left.

It took us a few minutes to get down from the trucks and prepare to head towards our new area. Victor did a roll call, and we began to unload bags for the move. Meir, who tried to stand up with his bag too quickly, didn't notice the pit behind him and fell on his back. We all stood up and started walking. While walking, I felt someone pushing me from behind. I turned around and straight away pushed him back! All the nerves from the slaps during the journey culminated in this moment. Kashi nearly fell backward. It turned out he had simply slipped and fallen towards me, and I pushed him in response. It was dangerous, he wasn't meant to be on the receiving end of my anger. He didn't mean to push me at all. I apologized. I explained to him that throughout the journey, someone had been slapping my head, and I thought it was him. "It's all good, Kuno, just relax a bit," he said. We continued to walk slowly towards the new strongholds. Every time you enter a new territory, you are more alert, but for some reason, I felt like the whole company had lost some of its operational alertness recently. A brief conversation with Yemini, and we both return to carry out the mission as needed. After walking a few hundred meters between buildings and fields, we reach our designated site.

The Feuer team begins to capture the basement floor, and we immediately go up to capture the rest of the floors. Upstairs, we realize it's a much larger building than we had expected, and that the upper floors are connected to the adjacent building, requiring us to clear and control it too. After half an hour of capturing, clearing, and scanning the building, we began to set up the stronghold. My hand still hurt, but I didn't let it affect me too much. When Nahman finished his briefing, I dozed off in less than a second. We only had one position, so the guard duty was also very short.

Monday, January 1, 2024

We woke up in the morning feeling refreshed. The atmosphere was good – a sense that it was our final moments in Gaza after a long period living without routine. We moved all the mattresses aside to give ourselves space to maneuver and waited to hear what was planned for us for the day. Amitai made a nice coffee from instant powder, and I settled down to play chess with Suedi. Nahman said that the Nahal Brigade was supposed to replace us in the evening, and until then, we have another mission to carry out in the zone. Everyone was eager to go out, so Meir pulled out his list. "Kuno and Yemini are staying," said Meir. "No way! No chance!" I replied immediately. "Not even Nahman will stop me." At first, the guys argued with me, until they realized they had no chance.

Suddenly, Meir started laughing. I asked him the reason for the laughter, but he wasn't prepared to answer me. I pushed him until he said, "Remember you got some whacks to the helmet yesterday? So there's a big chance it was me." He was lucky that my nerves had calmed from yesterday; otherwise, he might have found himself on the floor. "I wanted to tell you yesterday," he chuckled. "But after I saw how you pushed Kashi, I was petrified." We laughed together. It was decided that Yemini and Kaneti would stay to guard the stronghold together with the Feuer team's radio operator.

We began organizing equipment for the mission. Unpleasant as it may sound, one of my goals of this mission was to unload every possible gram from my backpack. I had approximately 20 explosive blocks, a detonation cord, prepared C-4 charges, a MAG bar, and more. It was clear to me that I wouldn't return with explosives from this mission. I made sure to take any remaining explosive gear from everyone else. Because Yemini, my demolition partner, was staying at the stronghold, I made a quick deal with Oz, not before I passed him some of the equipment. Oz's face lit up with a wide smile. It looked like he had been waiting for this for a long time.

We left. We began to advance down the street. Everything was very quiet, and we felt in control. I reminded myself that at any given moment, we could find ourselves in the middle of trouble.

There are several sites we need to search today, each belonging to a terrorist who participated in the events of October 7th. We enter to capture the first site, going floor by floor and clearing each apartment. During the scan of the second floor, we spot a body in advanced stages of decomposition in the backyard. "Lucky that the smell doesn't reach us here," I say to myself. I can no longer bear the stench of these bodies. We continue to scan the apartment up to the third floor. I stick my head out the window and glance quickly at the street. I spot a curtain flapping in the adjacent building. For a moment, I tried to work out whether it's just the wind, but an inner voice tells me to examine the window again. To my surprise, I identify next to the window a bald head with a white beard trying to peek and understand what's happening outside. A terrorist. Without hesitation, I aim the weapon towards the upper part of his chest, while updating Nahman about the terrorist identification. I request permission to fire, but Nahman prefers to check on the radio first to ensure it's not our forces. I wait. After a quick verification, we realize it indeed isn't our forces and decide to launch a team attack on the building.

Victor, Kashi, and I start firing towards the window while the rest of the team maneuvers and crosses the axis towards the site across the street. The rest of the team begins firing together with Rotem's operations commander. Nahman goes out with the Spear Squad and Oz towards the entrance of the building to open the door with explosives. After a short delay, they detonate the entrance. Oz's first explosion, the guy is pleased. We cease fire as the Spear Squad breaks into the site and starts scanning. Dotan and Shaked enter the building, not before Dotan prepares a grenade and throws it inside. They begin scanning the rooms, when suddenly a very old man with a white beard and a turban stands in front of them, raising his hands. Behind him is a body. It seems it has been here for a long time. The grenade Dotan threw didn't treat it well, to put it lightly. Very quickly, they pull the elderly man outside, hand him over to the operations commander, and continue scanning the building. At the same time, I look through the window and try to search for threats. We mustn't make any mistakes here. It's the last day, we can't do anything stupid. The guys finish the scan and leave, while Oz interrogates the older man and scans him for weapons and explosives. Then Oz brings him to us.

From the looks of it, the man is at least 85 years old. He speaks unclearly, though it could be either from fear or because he's trying to play us. Oz thinks he might be a bit crazy. He seemed very scared. Victor brought him a glass of water and made sure he was sitting comfortably. The team returned to the stronghold where we had identified him and we immediately began an investigation into this event. Oz said that from the conversation with the detainee, he understood that his brother was killed a month ago and since then he has stayed sitting next to him. It's no wonder he went crazy! Sitting for a month next to his brother's body, who wouldn't go crazy? Those who searched inside reported that there were birds in the room, or more accurately, pieces of birds. It seems that the man just ate them to survive.

In retrospect, I'm glad I didn't shoot him. Thank God everything went smoothly and no one was hurt, but at the same time, he could have been a terrorist and could have killed one of my comrades. If that had happened, I wouldn't have forgiven myself. If he'd been holding a Kalashnikov, he could have sprayed them at the entrance or detonated a charge. That's the complexity of war. It's terrible, bloody, but I'm not apologizing. I know very clearly what I'm doing here and why I'm here. When civilians and innocent people are killed, it's terrible and very sad, but it's largely the fault of Hamas which intentionally endangers its civilians. We go above and beyond to avoid killing civilians.

We moved the older man to the gathering point of the civilians and continued the mission. Moments before leaving the building, Suedi and I made sure to set it on fire. Let's say this time we didn't need to strain to see the building going up in flames. From there, we moved to an adjacent stronghold, met the Feuer team, said hi to them, and headed towards our next site – the building of a Hamas naval commando operative.

Just before we advanced towards his stronghold, we had to enter the building, and my eyes caught a picture hanging on the wall. An elderly woman around the age of 85 was standing and looking at the photographer, holding a Kalashnikov and looking through its scope. Unbelievable! I never imagined that such a picture would be hung on one of my grandmother's walls, but apparently among Gazans this is the model to imitate. An entire society that sanctifies death. When I go to my grandmother's house, I see pictures of grandchildren, or beautiful views and places in Israel.

Here, when a grandchild enters the house to hug their grandmother, the first picture he sees is of Grandma with a Kalashnikov. A bit shocked by the picture and all that it represented, we headed towards the next site. The door was locked. I explained to Oz how to blow up the entrance and let him lead. It didn't take much time to capture and scan the site. We found a wetsuit, weaponry, and a lot of Hamas military manuals.

I asked some guys to bring gas canisters from the surrounding sites while I marked the building's columns in order to knock down the house. Next to each column, I place a chair with a gas canister, and attach two explosive blocks to each balloon. I connect all the blocks to a central detonating cord, so that during the explosion, all the columns will collapse, followed by the entire house. Just before I finish, Nahman informs us that the Nahal soldiers are already walking around our zone, and we cannot detonate... What a shame!. If we can't blow it up, then let's at least burn it down. Explosive material is also very flammable, and there's no chance I'm returning with the explosives. I started scattering the explosive blocks throughout the house, and together with the team, we prepared the building for burning. Five minutes later, there wasn't much left of this house. The heat of the flames combined with the gas canisters and burning explosives did their job. We headed back towards the building, burning another house of a terrorist on the way. When we arrived at the site, we immediately removed our vests and let our bodies breathe a bit. Nahman announced that the 50th Battalion would arrive soon to relieve us. First, the Eshel and Feuer teams left, then Betzel and Atzits, and finally Kesten and us. The guys were cheerful. I was glad we let the Eshel team leave first; they deserved it.

I had mixed feelings. On one hand, I was happy that we were finishing our part in the war. We did so much and truly gave it our all. But on the other hand, the work isn't finished. I couldn't help but think about all the hostages, and the fact that Hamas still controls the area. Yes, they suffered a very hard blow, but there is still so much more to do.

In one of the resupplies we received in Al-Atatra, I found an improvised Cuban cigar on the floor made out of a plastic test tube. I was sure it belonged to someone, but I took it with me without any shame. I put it in my vest and told myself that on the day we finally leave Gaza, I would take the cigar out from my vest and smoke it together with the whole team. And so it was. I pulled out the cigar from my vest, and as I did, I suddenly heard from the side of the room, "Hey, scumbag! That's my cigar." Well, it turns out the cigar belongs to Suedi. We both laughed. Victor also pulled out a cigar, and we all began to smoke. Each took a puff, not before making sure they had a picture for a souvenir. There was an end-of-battle atmosphere. I laughed and said aloud, "End of a wet drill, end of the Gaza journey." We hope that the war will soon be over, and that we can safely bring all of the hostages back home.

The Eshel team was supposed to leave already, but to exit, they needed us to take their stronghold overlooking the Shati refugee camp. Nahman requested that six guys accompany him to replace them at the position until the Nahal soldiers arrived. I, successfully performing my task of unloading all of my explosives thus far, knew I had one task left: to unload all the MAG ammunition. I'm going back with an empty bag. I happily volunteered for the task, geared up, and made sure Meir brought his MAG. When we arrived at the Eshel team's building, we saw they were playing poker.

The guard shift passed quickly. There were several missile launches from the Shati direction, with background explosions of the Air Force, almost like a fireworks show that they arranged for my final exit from Gaza. Dotan arrived to replace me on guard duty, and I seized the moment for one final call from Gaza to Mom and Shiran, through Nurit's phone. When I finished the call, Battalion 50 arrived right on cue. I handed over to their demolition expert what little explosive gear remained, together with all the candies and snacks I had. We all took out everything good that we had left in our bags and gave it to them. It's the kind of camaraderie of soldiers that's hard to explain. Candies, socks, chess that accompanied us in the last period... It's difficult to describe this feeling, but it's most similar to a relay race. You know you've given your all, and now it's time to pass the baton to the next runner. Obviously, to win, you need to help him as much as you can. We didn't know anyone there, but we had so much in common. We encouraged them and wished them great success. I approached my bag for one last check before exiting. It had been a long time since my bag felt so light. But apparently, it wasn't the smartest thing to do since I ended up without explosives, without MAG ammo, without water, and without food. I made sure I had 7 full magazines for any unforeseen event, but apparently, it's never good to get to the brink. In war, you never know where you'll suddenly find yourself.

We left the building, stood in two rows, and Victor ran the roll call for the last time. Biton led, we followed him, with the Castan team behind us. As we walked, I reminded the guys next to me to pay attention to spacing and cover. We cannot fall at the last moment. I put on night vision goggles and looked up at the sky. It's a shame I couldn't capture this, it would have been an amazing picture! The sky was filled with waves of clouds. I know it sounds strange, like a weird expression. But I saw smoke clouds forming after the illuminating mortars that Hamas uses. In the background, the droning sound of diesel engines rose from the streets.

We advance towards the trucks waiting to take us back to Israel. The walk goes by quickly. This is the first time in the war that I'm walking with a bag and barely feel its weight. The Tatra trucks are waiting for us near a neighborhood of multi-story buildings. Luckily, this time we actually have 551 drivers, and more than that – each of us gets a seat. We settle into the seats, and the transfer fills up with bags. We haven't encountered such good treatment in a long time. We waited for about 20-25 minutes on the truck before we started moving. There's a sense of fulfillment in the air, but we try to maintain operational discipline as best as we can. Tzurieli sings one of the songs he wrote during the war with his team, and Suedi leads Michaeli's cover of *Resisim*[45] that we wrote after the incident with the Snippe team. As we begin to move, as we distance ourselves from the outskirts

---

45 A famous song in Israel by Raviv Kaner.

of Gaza City and approach the border, the atmosphere on the truck gets more excitable. As we see the border approaching, we start to roar:

10
9
8
7
6
5
4
3
2
1

We stand on the truck seats with our weapons in the air and flashlights. The moment we crossed the border, we burst into the song we sang when we were released from the army: "I searched for love all my life, I was sailing on a drifting ship. I crossed continents and seas..."

Everyone is shouting, singing, and getting excited. I glance to the sides and realize that the entire convoy of Tatra trucks had joined us in the singing. Hundreds of soldiers are standing on the truck seats and singing powerfully. They're shooting laser beams into the sky and throwing glow sticks into the air.

We are the last soldiers of our brigade in Gaza. Everyone is waiting for us. The battalion is waiting for the end of the battle ceremony in Zikim.

As we enter the parking lot, we start chanting and jumping on the trucks, singing loudly. There isn't a single person indifferent to the sight of hundreds of soldiers returning from Gaza full of energy and joy. Hundreds of combat and support soldiers who waited for us for the ceremony immediately took out their phones and captured this moment. In the background, songs of faith, hope and victory blasted from the speakers, turning the moment into an unforgettable one. Like in a parade, the truck drivers continued to drive in circles in the parking lot until they stopped and parked in place.

I was filled with happiness! I simply started dancing and crying tears of joy. What a privilege we have to all come out of the war healthy and whole. The company sergeants immediately came over to say hi, and Dekel made sure to capture a picture of the end of the battle. We received our phones, and I quickly called Shiran to update her that we had got out. My battery was dead, and the phone switched off, but I was happy about it. I wanted to live in the moment, to feel it, to be a part of this great thing. I saw that I'm not the only crazy one. Dozens of other soldiers started dancing to the melody of the music and songs. Friends hugged, some cried, but I didn't stop dancing and jumping. We made sure all the equipment was returned, and we ate the burgers they brought for us. Over the loudspeakers, we were called to gather for a ceremony. The base commander asked everyone to put on combat gear, but bursts of laughter sounded throughout the parking lot. It didn't seem like anyone was planning on putting on vests for some ceremony, with all due respect.

It was a special ceremony. First, they showed the speech of the battalion commander on the radio right before the exit from Gaza:

"Moses Stations, this is your commander speaking. On October 7th, the Hamas murderers left Beit Hanoun, Beit Lahiya, Jabaliya, and Shati, and brought great darkness. That same night, we all stood together like lions to bring back the light. We reached each one of these places. We killed hundreds of terrorists, destroyed dozens of tunnels, returned a number of our murdered for burial in Israel, and destroyed four of the enemy's most significant command units...

Today, we conclude 87 days of combat. 87 days of camaraderie and mutual guarantee. We are ready to return and take up the fight again – in the North, South, and anywhere else, until the job is done.

Be proud of yourselves.

Today we are embarking on another mission – to bring the message of unity to the homefront. Unity isn't just "quiet, we're shooting." True unity is listening, persuading, compromising, settling debates, and most importantly, moving forward together. That is victory."

It was very emotional. The battalion commander himself spoke, followed by the brigade commander. They mentioned the names of those who fell in the battalion – Tzvika Lavi, Gal Meir Eisenkot, and Eyal Meir Berkowitz. Even amidst the great joy, no one forgot them for a single moment.

The battalion ceremony concluded, and Rotem gathered us for a final summary discussion before heading home. The guys were already a bit tired, but I think he spoke beautifully. Rotem summarized briefly the process we had gone through from the seventh of October until now. All the challenges we faced along the way, "until the moment the last soldier's foot stepped off the truck onto Israeli soil." I saw how emotional it was for him to see the entire company standing together. During the war, we had all sorts of moments of disagreement, and sometimes even moments of deep tensions. But in the end, the entire battalion is here together, healthy and whole, after fulfilling all their missions, and for that, I take my hat off to him. I approached Rotem and personally thanked him for a challenging and complex period and for the great privilege that fell in my lot, to fight in the 551st Brigade.

We boarded the buses that were heading to Bilu. On the way, I thought about all the friends who fell. Some I knew briefly, others were true friends. Some were my soldiers, some were commanders. One thing was common to all: they were the best, the most special, whose absence was keenly felt especially in the great moment of release, and will continue to accompany us for many years to come. I know we will never forget for what cause they fell, and against which enemy they fought bravely.

And now, there is a new mission. Not a mission announced by Nahman, but a mission that each one of us feels deep in our bones: Unity among the people.

In memory of my friends who fell in battle:

Avi Buzaglo
10/07/23, fell in battle in Ofakim

Ben Bronstein
10/07/23, fell in battles for the Gaza Envelope communities

May Naim
10/07/23, murdered at the Nova music festival

Gaya Halifa
10/07/23, murdered at the Nova music festival

Yotam Ben Bassat
10/07/23, fell in battles for the Gaza Envelope communities

Aryeh Shlomo Ziering
10/07/23, fell in battles for the Gaza Envelope communities

Omri Michaeli
10/07/23, fell in battles for the Gaza Envelope communities

Roy Yosef Levy
10/07/23, fell in battles for the Gaza Envelope communities

Eliad Ohayon
10/07/23, murdered in Ofakim

Yehuda Natan Cohen
11/03/23, fell in battle in northern Gaza

Moshe Yedidyah Leiter
11/10/23, fell in battle in northern Gaza

Sergey Shmerkin
11/10/23, fell in battle in northern Gaza

Matan Meir
11/10/23, fell in battle in northern Gaza

Yosef Chaim Hershkowitz
11/10/23, fell in battle in northern Gaza

Yedidya Asher Lev
11/14/23, fell in battle in northern Gaza

Eyal Meir Berkowitz
12/07/23, fell in battle in northern Gaza

Gal Meir Eisenkot
12/07/23, fell in battle in northern Gaza

Tzvika Lavi
12/11/23 died from his injuries after combat in northern Gaza

Etan Naeh
12/17/23, fell in battle in southern Gaza

Liav Elosh
12/17/23, fell in battle in southern Gaza

Daniel Ben Harosh
12/18/23, fell in battle in the northern Gaza

Maoz Fenigstein
12/19/23, fell in battle in the northern Gaza

Shauli Greenglick
12/26/23, fell in battle in the northern Gaza

Shay Shamriz
12/26/23, fell in battle in the northern Gaza

Dvir Pima
12/27/23, fell in battle in the northern Gaza

Dan Weidenbaum
01/12/24, fell in battle in central Gaza

Itay Seif
02/27/24, fell in battle in northern Gaza

May their memories be a blessing.